INTENTIONAL
RELATIONSHIPS

FAMILIUS

Published by Familius LLC, www.familius.com

Familius books are available at special discounts for bulk purchases, whether for sales promotions or for family or corporate use. For more information, contact Familius Sales at 559-876-2170 or email orders@familius.com.

Library of Congress Cataloging-in-Publication Data
2015955940

Print ISBN 9781942934479
Ebook ISBN 9781944822118
Hardcover ISBN 9781944822125

Printed in the United States of America

Edited by Lindsay Sandberg
Cover design by David Miles
Book design by Brooke Jorden

10 9 8 7 6 5 4 3 2 1
First Edition

INTENTIONAL
RELATIONSHIPS

HOW TO WORK
AND SUCCEED WITH
OTHERS

KEN TUCKER

DEDICATION

1. Relationships fuel not who you have been but who you are becoming.
2. You are exactly who your relationships demonstrate that you are.
3. In our fast-paced society, relationship gets left along the way.

These are three lessons my most important relationships have taught me—relationships with my wife, Judy; my children, Kendra, Kristen, and Kenny; my children-in-law, Tony and Lizzy; and my grandchildren, Madelyn and James Montgomery.

These same lessons have been reinforced by my colleagues at TAG Consulting—these are the teachers, the influencers whose voices play in my head and heart as I write this book.

My intent is to awaken and reinforce the good and useful lessons about relationships you have learned through your family, friends, and colleagues.

CONTENTS

PREFACE

study relationships. I am an executive coach; every day my job is to help leaders in industry, government, faith-based communities, healthcare, and education develop and nurture healthy relationships at work and at home. With my colleagues, we collectively have more than one hundred years of experience studying and helping to improve the relationships of thousands of executives, managers, employees, husbands, wives, children, and friends.

We are certified consultants, licensed professionals, practicing hands-on technicians, and, most importantly, learners. With every new assignment and every new client, I start by learning their business, culture, customers, products, and service—and I assess the health of the relationships that exist within the organization. What I learn about the organization and the relationships therein I use to teach executives, managers, and employees how to increase their relationship effectiveness at work and at home.

In this book, I share a key concept of any relationship that I have learned from studying multiple organizations and coaching hundreds of individuals about relationship: success comes from how those in a relationship choose to behave. The simple and practical premise of this book is: change your behavior and you will change your relationship.

Let me be clear. Relationships are not just romantic relationships. You have a relationship with every person you encounter: a colleague, an employer, a child, a spouse, an in-law, etc. And because we have so many relationships, it is important to make sure that we behave in such a way that maintains healthy relations.

I will use examples I've seen in my work with building workplace relationships to show you how to change any relationship for the better. These examples become a metaphor for how we each behave with our family, friends, and neighbors. As you read the workplace examples, be thinking of how your personal relationships could benefit from changing your behavior as the people in the stories do.

So "How do you behave?" is an important question—one this book asks each reader to consider. This book's purpose is to teach you how to be the best you can be in all of your relationships. That makes this a *how-to* book. It is about how to practice relationship in a way that transforms your current relationship with your spouse, siblings, supervisor, subordinates, and friends into an intentional relationship. It is about how to practice relationship in a way that increases connection with your parents, brothers, and sisters. It is about how to develop relationships in a way that increases your effectiveness as a manager. It is about how to facilitate relationships in a way that increases the number of people you work with successfully. It is about how to cultivate relationships with your manager and coworkers in a way that increases the productivity of the team. And it is about how to be the best friend you can be to your friends.

How, then, will this book help you do and be all of this? By doing one thing—teaching you how to turn existing relationships into *intentional relationships*. An intentional relationship is the *uplifting use of personality, conversation, insight, opinion, and influence to create and maintain a mutual and selfless connection.*

In my last book, *Intentional Conversations: How to Rethink Everyday Conversations and Transform Your Career*, readers learned how to use conversation in a different and life-impacting way. In this book, you will learn how to behave in ways that reveal the unique and indispensable value you bring to every relationship. Relationship, I believe, is something we do, not something that happens on its own.

So how do you behave now in your relationships?

Are you choosy about your relationships—as choosy as Google is about who they hire? Google, according to Laszlo Bock in his book *Work Rules!*, is twenty-five times more selective than Harvard, Yale, or Princeton. Out of the more than two million who apply for jobs at Google every year, Bock writes, only 15,000 or one out of every 130 people get hired.[1]

Are you spontaneous in your relationships—as spontaneous as the online shoe supplier Zappos is? Zappos employees are trained to be spontaneous with customers. One famous story is told about a customer calling the Zappos call center thinking they were calling a pizza delivery service. The employee along with the manager proceeded to arrange for a pizza to be delivered by making the call for the customer.

Are you devoted to serving others in your relationships—as devoted as the high-end clothing store Nordstrom is? Their employees are known to live and demonstrate the store's mantra, "to serve and be kind" to everyone, from the affluent wealthy customer to the lowly homeless person living on the streets.

Can you end relationships decisively—as decisively as GE has been known to do? Jack Welch, former CEO, was notorious for the abrupt and efficient dismissal of employees, regardless of tenure, whose performance measured in the bottom 10 percent.

Throughout this book, I offer opportunities for you to evaluate how you behave in each of your relationships and ways to adjust your behavior and take advantage of opportunities so that your relationships become intentional and plentiful.

Cheryl and I get along really well. I consider her one of my best friends at work. I know she will be 100 percent on board with me being her new CEO. Of course, she will have to take on more responsibility than before, but that comes with the territory of being a COO. She will be the first one to step up to the plate to support me and do even more than she has in the past.

—MARK

I really don't trust him to lead our company. I know that is a harsh thing to say, but Mark just does not instill in me the confidence that I had in our last CEO. Although he and I are good friends, he does not demonstrate that he understands enough about the business to lead us successfully. I do not think I will stay with the company now that he is taking over.

—CHERYL

CHAPTER ONE

VINTAGE YOU: DOING YOU IN RELATIONSHIPS

RELATIONSHIP IS WHAT YOU DO REPEATEDLY.

"Do you think you could benefit from a relationship assistant?" I asked a regional sales manager from Toyota USA as he was sitting across from me. He instantly recoiled, obviously upset by my question.

"Why do you say that?" he asked.

"How do you," I replied, taking a different track, "benefit now from your administrative assistant?"

His face softened a bit as he proceeded to tell me how his assistant helps to keep him organized, helps him to be on time for meetings, keeps him aware of client needs, and schedules time with his direct reports and about multiple other ways she was a support to him. "Overall," he concluded, now fully engaged in the conversation, "she really is a good partner to me; she has skills and knowledge that complement who I am."

"So I hear you saying," I gently interjected, "that she comes alongside of you and helps you to be more effective, right?"

"Absolutely," he said, nodding his head. "She is much better at dealing with persistent, complaining individuals than I am. I don't handle the 'people stuff' like that with as much finesse as she does," he replied.

"Well, she is who I had in mind when I mentioned a relationship assistant for you. She understands people in a way that could really help you be even more effective as a leader," I said to him.

Instead of responding to my last words, he stood up, reached out, and quickly shook my hand, indicating that we were done. I took that to mean he had no interest in pursuing my suggestion.

That is how we left it, until more than a year later when to my delight he told me this story about that same assistant:

> "They call you Crickets," my assistant said to me. "Yes, Crickets, like when it is so quiet you can hear the sound of crickets. You don't talk to them," she said quietly. "Just talk to them."
>
> I was stunned and a bit indignant. "That's it? Talk to them?"
>
> "Yes," she said. "Every morning, you walk past your entire staff sitting at their desks without saying a word to anyone. Then, at lunchtime, you repeat it all over again. The only time you speak to them is when you have a request or some job-related subject to discuss."

That conversation with my assistant changed my career and, in many ways, changed my life. You see, a few days after that jarring conversation, I decided to change. I did not want to be Crickets.

I am a list-maker; anything that I put on my list for the day gets done. So, every day now, I write down on my list "Get water" twice. Once in the morning and once in the afternoon as I leave my office to get water to drink, I stop and talk with an employee, and on the way back, I stop and speak with another employee. The results over the last twelve months have been remarkable. My decisions about the team and our work are far more informed. Now I know almost immediately when an employee discovers a new way to solve a work-related problem, whereas in the past I never would have been included in the spontaneous shoptalk.

This manager had been unaware of his behavior—that is, until he got some relationship assistance from his assistant. "How do you behave in your relationships?" asked within the world of family, friends, coworkers, and supervisors becomes a revealing and compelling personal question. For how you choose to behave in relationships has tremendous impact upon the degree of happiness in your marriage, on the lasting influence of your parental advice, on whether or not your presence is valued at work, and on the durability of your friendships.

When you recognize your behavior, it reveals who you truly are—how you "do you." How you do you is displayed in the why, if, and when you ask someone to marry you. It is expressed in your response to your self-actualizing, individuating teenager. It is present in how you treat subordinates. It prescribes how you get work done with coworkers. It informs how you celebrate a friend's success. How you use self, how you choose to be you, is crucial to your relationships. All of your relationships—those with your manager, mother, or mate—are all influenced by how you do you.

Each individual influences the nature of the relationship by what they do. How you do you with me and how I do me with you is the sum total of our relationship. Sadly, we are often unintentional in our use of our truest self.

This is the grand challenge: to learn how to behave in an intentional way that enhances relationship outcomes. To do this, we must increase our self-awareness, as stated by Charles N. Seashore, Mary Nash Shawver, Greg Thompson, and Marty Mattare in their article "Doing Good by Knowing Who You Are: The Instrumental Self As an Agent of Change":

> Self-awareness is the foundational concept of use of self. Just as all craftspeople must know their tools, all musicians must know their instruments, all facilitators of individual change must first know themselves as an instrument of change . . . intentional use of self "starts with our understanding of who we are, our conscious perception of our Self."[2]

Becoming aware of how it is you behave and how to behave differently—intentionally—brings reward both for you and for others. Like the manager for Toyota, you may be damaging relationships by how you are coming across to others. The good news is that you can almost immediately improve the quality of all your relationships by becoming more aware of how you are impacting important relationships at work and home. There are times when we have no clue how we may be coming across to the other person. This lack of awareness of how our behavior impacts the other person is a silent but deadly killer in relationships. Whether we realize their impact or not, relationships thrive or die due to our repeated behavior.

The best way to improve your marriage—and I would say any relationship—is as Paul Tripp, author of *What Did You Expect? Redeeming the Realities of Marriage*, has said: "to draw a circle around you, and work on everybody in that circle."[3]

Working on how you act toward others starts with you recognizing the area(s) of behavior you need to change. The assistant recognized the negative impact the manager's behavior was having upon his staff. And even with a little coaching from his assistant, nothing would have been different unless he took charge of his own behavior. Nobody can change the way you behave in relationships but you. And it's up to you to be aware of how you doing you with your supervisor, coworkers, direct reports, spouse, children, or friends is helping or hurting your relationship with them. How you do you is a personal choice. You decide how you use self—and you get the rewards or suffer the loss by what you do.

With all that can be said about relationships, there is one thing that needs to be stressed: relationships thrive or die based upon how you do you. Relationships are tried, proven, and often destroyed by our use of self. Self is our personal, 24/7 tool to use. We have a lifetime of experience with its use. And yet somehow, "self" may be the one instrument we use callously, ineffectively, inefficiently, and unintentionally. This disuse and misuse of self is to our harm and that of others.

If we choose, we can change the way we use self in our relationships. That is one thing you will learn how to do in this book:

how to behave with purpose in an uplifting way in all of your relationships.

Are there relationships you would like to enhance? Maybe the one you have with your spouse, child, or sibling? Or is it one at work, with your supervisor, coworker, or customer? Whichever one you want to work on, you can start by catching what you do in relationships. Like the manager in the example, you will benefit from a "relationship assistant."

A relationship assistant is someone you trust and to whom you have given permission and invitation to observe you in your relationships. Let me use a recent example to illustrate what I am saying.

> My wife, Judy, and I were out doing our almost-daily evening walk, except on this day, we started out running for a bit. As we ran, we came across two older ladies walking (that is not to say we are spring chickens ourselves) who greeted us heartily as we ran by them. We returned the greetings and proceeded on. About an hour later, we met the same ladies again, but this time, we were walking. Upon seeing us, a short conversation ensued:
>
> Ladies: Hi there, again.
>
> Judy and Ken: Hello, again.
>
> Ladies: So, last time we saw you, you were running. What happened?
>
> Ken: The running was only to show off. As soon as we were out of your sight, we stopped.
>
> Ladies, Judy, and Ken: (Laughter.)
>
> Later that evening after our walk, as we were settling down for the night, I asked Judy, "When was the last time you caught you doing you?"

She thought for a few moments and said she did not know. But then she said, "I can tell you exactly when last I saw you doing you."

I laughed. "You think so?"

"Today when we were walking," she continued, "you were vintage you. It was fun observing how quickly we connected with our neighbors because of your personality. Your 'Woo talent theme' made it a very pleasant exchange," she concluded.

Moments like these happen—those times when you behave in a way that is "vintage" you, when your behavior is so you that it is obvious to someone who knows you. These moments are poignantly instructive for us, moments when a relationship assistant (in my case, my wife) can help us see what we do in relationships.

In your present relationships, how are you behaving? At home, how are you doing you? At work, what results are you getting from how you do you? Do you know? You need to know. For to work and succeed with others, you must understand the impact of your repeated behavior upon relationships; you must understand how to use your vintage self.

Relationships are dynamic and complex. Sometimes, we are effective in them. Many times, we are not. Part of the complexity of relationships is how numerous and diverse they can be. There are family-ships, within which you are required to behave in a way that maintains intimacy with your spouse, to render support to your children, at times to be a confidant for a relative, and so on. There are friendships, within which you may be required to be a counselor for your best friend, the Saturday-barbecue chef for your neighbors, or the timekeeper for the acquaintance at the gym.

Then there are workplace-ships, where you have a subordinate role to your manager, or you are the hang-out-together-after-work-friend with a teammate, or you have a chat-at-the-water-cooler friendship with a coworker, and so on. Whatever the type of relationship, these things are likely to be true:

- Relationships exist and end by what you do.
- Relationships are responsive to what you do.
- Relationships are healthy or unhealthy, at least partially, because of what you do.
- Relationships, because of what you do, help or hinder you in the achievement of personal and organizational goals.

When was the last time you were consciously aware that you were being "vintage" you? What were you doing? How did your behavior impact your relationship? Did it bring about a positive or negative result?

So, how do you behave? What can you do to increase your relationship effectiveness?

Playing "alligator water"—that comes to mind when I think of my dad sometimes. It was a silly game that he made up when we were kids. It involved jumping on the furniture so the alligator, my playful dad, didn't catch us. We would play this game for hours in the basement of our rented home. He was so fun, the childish one of our parents. That was before he grew up and became an angry man, distant and withdrawn from us.

—DAUGHTER

The earliest memory I have of my second daughter always includes her bubbly laughter. Light-hearted and effervescent *are words that describe her personality. I alternated between using "Precious" and "Bubbly" as endearing names for her. Strangely as I write this, I am nostalgic for those early childhood days when she was my little girl. I miss that person, the one who needed me and wanted me to take care of her. I miss it even more because I have come to realize over the years just how stingy and selective I was with showing my love for her.*

—FATHER

CHAPTER TWO

UNFORGETTABLE YOU: ETCHING YOU INTO RELATIONSHIPS

RELATIONSHIP IS WHAT IS REMEMBERED AND VALUED.

I was writing a *Gallup Journal* article entitled "A Passion for Work" when I felt I should include a real life illustration of what passion at work looked like. I sat there momentarily stumped until a thought occurred to me. I picked up the phone and dialed the Southwest Airlines 1-800 number. A man answered the phone.

Ken: Hello, my name is Ken Tucker, and I am writing an article for a business journal about passion at work. Do you have any personal examples that you have witnessed of people who are passionate about their work?

Southwest employee: Hmmm. I don't know what you mean.

Ken: Thank you; no problem. Sorry to have bothered you.

(I hung up the phone and pressed redial. This time, a woman named Monica answered the phone.)

Ken: Hello, my name is Ken Tucker, and I am writing an article for a business journal about passion at work. Do you have any personal examples that you have witnessed of people who are passionate about their work?

Monica: How much time you got?

Ken (laughing): As much time as you need.

Monica: I was traveling on Southwest Airlines when I had an experience that I will never forget. In fact, this experience helped me to make a very important life decision.

(Monica went on to relate how as she was waiting to board a flight, she saw a little girl crying. As a flight attendant comforted her, Monica gathered that she was traveling alone and had been worried about leaving her mother. Later, during the flight, from her seat across the aisle, Monica saw that the girl was crying again. The flight attendant did something "absolutely amazing," Monica recalled.)

Monica: The flight attendant, clearly, had already devised a plan on how she would help the little girl—she pulled out her credit card and helped the girl use the telephone on the back of the chair before her to call her grandparents. As I eavesdropped, I surmised that her grandparents assured her they would be waiting for her when the plane landed. The little girl was comforted and was fine for the rest of the flight.

Ken: Monica, that is really a good story!

Monica (emphatically, with humor in her voice): I am not done yet.

Ken: Please, go on; tell me more.

Monica: That little girl's world was positively changed because of that attendant. So was mine. That was the moment I decided to accept the job Southwest had offered me.

Ken: Thank you, Monica, for sharing that story with me.

Monica: It's been two and a half years since that day, and Southwest continues to be a great place for me to work.

The flight attendant scored by impacting two lives that day. She took advantage of what we call a Relationship-Impacting Opportunity, a RIO (pronounced *ree-oh*). She scored the first one with that little girl, and in doing so, took customer service to another level that day. She scored the second by creating a positive memory for Monica. That is one of the crucial things about RIOs—once you score, it has the power to inspire others. Every day, just like the Southwest flight attendant, we are afforded daily interactions which present RIOs to us. It is up to us to behave in a way to turn them into positive memories.

The nature and longevity of relationships are impacted by events that are remembered and treasured. Events such as disconnects and disappointments, although mostly unintended, happen often in relationships. We do not intend for this to happen, but sometimes, our relationships at home or at work fail. We do not mean to lose connection with our family member, friends, supervisor, or customers.

But what can we do to prevent this from happening? Is there something we can be doing to enhance our relationships? Yes, absolutely! Relationship, as we wrote in the last chapter, is about what you do. And what you do creates memories that define your relationships. Every day, there are potential memory-creating events—RIOs—that occur in which how we behave determines whether a relationship grows, falters, or dies. Let me illustrate with one of my fondest memories as a customer.

One day, my phone buzzed just as I got off the plane at Dulles Washington International Airport. It was a voicemail from my assistant, Diane, informing me that my connecting flight had been canceled. This was a big problem, she informed me, because all of the rental cars in the DC area were sold out due to the upcoming holiday weekend. As I finished listening to her voicemail, I looked at my watch and saw that it was 4:30 p.m. I cringed. The thought of disappointing hundreds of people troubled me.

I sat down at the nearby waiting area and used my phone to look up the distance between the airport and Hershey, Pennsylvania— it turned out to be a mere two-and-half-hour drive, I was happy to discover. I could drive there in time for my speech—if only I had a car. I was determined to get there somehow, so I headed toward the shuttle to the rental car companies. As I boarded the bus and sat down, I pulled out my Hertz Gold Number One card to get the phone number. As I looked at the card, the "member since" line gave me an idea. It told me that I had been renting cars from Hertz for five years. I dialed Hertz Rental Cars, and after a long list of automated options, I finally got Suzie, a reservations agent, on the phone. This is how the conversation proceeded:

Hertz employee: Hertz Number One Gold service, this is Suzie. May I have your name, please?

Ken: Hello, my name is Ken Tucker, and I am a Hertz Gold Number One customer. My assistant has already told me you are sold out of cars, but I thought I would call and let you know that this is your opportunity to make me a Hertz customer for life.

Suzie (laughing): So tell me exactly where you are.

Ken: I am at Dulles Airport on the bus headed to your lot, and I need a car now or I will likely lose a client and disappoint three hundred people. That is why this is your opportunity to make me a Hertz customer for life. Can you help me, please?

Suzie: Mr. Tucker, it is showing that we are sold out completely of cars at that location, but stay on the line while I try to find a way to help you.

(Eight minutes later as the bus pulled into the Hertz lot, Suzie came back on the phone.)

Suzie: Mr. Tucker, have you arrived there yet?

Ken: Yes, I am just getting off the bus.

Suzie: As you exit the bus, head toward the front door of the customer service office. You will find a white Land Rover Discovery. That is your car, sir. It is brand new with less than twenty miles on it. It is one of a new delivery of cars that has not been put into service yet. Would that work for you?

Ken: Yes, absolutely. Thank you so much, and as I

promised, you have made me a Hertz customer for life.

I took the car, drove just less than 10 miles *above* the speed limit, and made it on time for my speech. That was July 1999, and on every trip since, just like I promised, I have only rented cars from Hertz. Suzie did a good thing for me that day. More importantly, she behaved in a way that I will never forget.

Now I have offered you two examples of using RIOs to enhance work relationships, specifically that of employee-customer relationships, but what does that mean for other relationships? What about family relationships? It changes everything! When you recognize and take advantage of RIOs in a family-ship, you strengthen each other and become closer.

Jack (one of my longest and closest friends) and I were talking over the phone one day when I asked him what he was doing at the moment. He told me he was in the kitchen preparing dinner for him and his wife so that it would be ready for when she arrived home from work. His comment changed the nature and purpose of my call from just a casual check-in with my best buddy to one of research and insight.

As we continued our chat, I followed up by asking him why he was preparing the dinner. He explained that it made sense as he was the one that arrived home from work earlier. We wrapped up our conversation and hung up.

Let me back up a little to provide some context before telling you the rest of the story and its relevance to this book. Jack and I have been best friends for years. We remained close through his first marriage and divorce, through his second marriage and divorce, and through his third marriage and divorce. We have cried together, prayed together, and rejoiced together. I know Jack well, as he does me.

Jack and I had worked through our call that day by covering just the usual updates around "How was your day?" and "What are your plans for tomorrow?" However, at 5 o'clock the next morning, it hit me. I jumped up and called Jack back. This is how that conversation went:

Ken: Jack, you are amazing! Absolutely incredible!

(Remember, he knows me and he is used to me).

Jack (in a bland, unimpressed voice): So what did I do now?

Ken: You are doing you differently!

Jack: Huh?

Ken: You never cook. You never think to cook. In thirty years of friendship, I have always known you to expect your wife to cook and serve you.

Jack: That's true in the past. But these days, I get home early to cook dinner so Gwen does not have to worry about doing that when she comes home tired.

Ken: Jack, you are amazing! That was a Relationship-Impacting Opportunity!

Jack: A what?

Ken: A RIO. There are three things you can choose to do with an opportunity to impact a relationship—you just chose to do the positive one. You see, you can score, you can forfeit, or you can ignore it. You just scored. RIO stands for Relationship-Impacting Opportunity. By cooking for your wife, you embraced the opportunity to positively impact your relationship with her. You are scoring big right now, my friend; you are scoring big.

Jack: (Silence. A very long silence.)

Ken: Jack, you still there?

Jack: Yeah . . . I was just thinking, *Why didn't I do this before?* I just realized in this moment that I could have chosen to do things like this before, but didn't—at least, not in any of my first three marriages.

That call with Jack did two things for me that day. First, his parting reflection sobered me. I was sobered because I know I miss RIOs all the time with my wife, my children, my employees, and my business partners. Second, his cooking for his wife inspired me—I immediately made a plan to score a RIO with my wife when she came home. I got home early enough that day to cook dinner for her, just like Jack had done.

That is another crucial thing about RIOs: we do not have to wait for them to happen—we can actually choose to make them happen. We build relationship by creating a positive memory, either intentionally, like planning to make a spouse dinner, or spontaneously, like the flight attendant's kindness to a passenger.

Relationship-Impacting Opportunities occur multiple times every day. They are present every time we interact with a person with whom we have some sort of relationship. The relationship may be employee to client, as in the case with me and the Hertz representative and the flight attendant and the little girl. The relationship may be with a family member, as in the example of Jack with his wife, or it may be a friendship, such as Jack and I have. The relationship may also be among coworkers. Every RIO impacts your existing relationships in some way or another. We can score RIOs by doing something that positively impacts our relationship. Or we can, sad to say, ignore or forfeit RIOs by choosing not to do something positive or behaving in a way that negatively impacts our relationship. But know this: ignore or forfeit a RIO at your own peril—your relationships will inevitably suffer.

In the following chapters, we will follow the progression of a company that had a culture and a history of forfeiting RIOs, but for now, let me highlight five things to consider about Relationship-Impacting Opportunities:

- RIOs occur every day
- RIOs are cumulative
- RIOs determine the quality of your relationships
- RIOs tell people what to expect from you
- RIOs strengthen, weaken, or destroy relationships

Relationships are an accumulation of Relationship-Impacting Opportunities and whether or not we behave in a way to turn them into good or bad memories. So how are RIOs working out for you? Looking back on a recent RIO, based upon your behavior, is it likely a good or bad memory of you? Are there relationships you know you can improve? Of course!

You can make any relationship, at work or at home, stronger by recognizing those memory-building moments of impact and scoring big with the people you care about and respect.

I just wish he would listen to me more. I feel he is always busy with everyone else, anything else, other than with me. I may as well just be alone. After all, I am mostly that way now. He is gone all the time, and when he is here, he never really listens to me or shares what is on his mind.

—WIFE

She talks all the time. Nonstop. I just wish she would just ease up on complaining. As soon as I step into the house from work or from a long, tiring trip, she starts right in on how the washing machine broke, or her sister had another fight with her boyfriend, or the kids were misbehaving. Every time she speaks, it is to whine about something.

—HUSBAND

CHAPTER THREE

UNDENIABLE YOU: REVEALING YOUR INTENTIONS IN RELATIONSHIPS

RELATIONSHIP IS A CHOICE.

More than a decade ago, a team and I worked with a CEO and executive team of an emergency services company. Our assignment was to help this team build a more collaborative and engaging workplace. On the surface, it was a simple enough assignment: do some conflict resolution training and six months of executive coaching for the leadership team followed up by a few team-building events so people should be ready to work together.

It was not to be. Through this organization and the variety of relationship situations that would happen therein, we were about to learn a very painful lesson about how when RIOs are ignored or forfeited, they can lead to disastrous results for all parties.

The Board had contacted us directly because of the alleged behavior of the executive team. The team was led by Tom, the CEO: a focused, authoritative, no-nonsense type of person who routinely asserted his power. As it was, this was part of the reason why the Board reached out to us for help. They were informed by several employees that Tom was using his position and authority as CEO in an intimidating and demeaning way. The Board, at the same time, had also been informed by persons on the executive team that Tom was coddling and protecting some who were misusing position and authority.

The Board was unsure who or what to believe. They had hired Tom and had found him to be very effective in increasing profits. He had introduced new strategies, products, and services effectively. As far as they were concerned, they wanted to expend every effort they could to correct whatever the situation was and, if appropriate, retain Tom as CEO.

The Board hired us to assess the situation and return to them with one of three recommendations: terminate Tom, remediate and coach Tom, or leave Tom in place and terminate other individuals on the executive team.

We made our recommendation—with a twist—based upon what we discovered through interviews and focus groups. The data we collected revealed that there were multiple relationships across the organization, most of them (regrettably) negative, exclusive, and adversarial towards people who were not already in the group.

Tom, his deputy, and the human resources director formed a clique.

The sales manager and two of the other division managers made up a clique.

The employees in the Kalamazoo area made up a clique.

The employees in the Houston area made up another clique.

Individuals were loyal to whatever clique they belonged to and unhelpful, even hostile, toward others. This was relationship gone amuck.

Back then, in 2005, whenever we worked with an organization, like Tom's, that was experiencing interpersonal and team conflict, we took a team-building, conflict-resolution approach. The tried and proven solution to dysfunction within a workgroup or organization was to teach and train the manager and their team what it meant to be a part of a team.

So we were fully prepared, based upon what the Board had told us, to work with an organization whose workgroups just needed to learn how to work together. Instead, we found an organization with territorial and adversarial gangs that bred widespread distrust and nepotism. The anger, animosity, and hostility created a veritable war zone in this workplace. Lines were drawn between workgroups that pitted manager against manager and teams against teams.

This revelation forced us to come up with a different approach from that which we had planned to use. None of the three suggested recommendations applied: firing Tom would not remove the widespread animosity and distrust among the staff; coaching Tom alone would be an insufficient response to bring about the wholesale change required; and leaving Tom in place and terminating any individual on the executive team would only lead individual workgroups to feel like their leader was being unfairly singled out, creating even more distrust. Instead, we realized that this was going to require more than the usual intervention strategies. Pervasive and pivotal change was needed. That change, we decided, had to include the dismantling of the disruptive relationships Tom and his leadership team had fostered and enabled.

What did we recommend? First, we recommended that everyone be retained in his or her job—we believed that nobody needed to get fired (at least, not yet).

Second, and most importantly, we recommended that Tom and his team be given a new bonus structure. Okay, so you have to admit, that is a twist. Here we have an organization on the brink of civil war, and we are recommending bonuses for the leaders that created the chaos. We did. We suggested tying the bonuses, which Tom and his team were used to getting every quarter, to measurable improvement in the relationships across the organization—an incentive to make relationship-building a priority. The Board expressed some concern about rewarding "bad behavior" but then accepted our recommendation and hired us to do the work.

It turned out that the work was like nothing we had ever done before. Never before had we insisted that an organization shift its efforts and incentives to focus primarily on fixing interpersonal relationships. When there are interpersonal conflicts in an organization, the problem is usually isolated within a workgroup or between individuals who are having personality clashes. In most instances, as I mentioned above, conducting team-building and/or coaching sessions quickly resolved the situations so people could get back to work.

This was different, drastically different. The entire organization was embroiled in relationship fallout at some level in every department. No executive, manager, or employee was exempt from having some relationship problem with at least one other group. The level of hurt feelings and cronyism was toxic. By connecting how executives got paid to how they and their teams interacted, we made relationship a central consideration to a company known for prejudicial and exclusive relationships.

The data we collected from surveys, focus groups, and one-on-one interviews revealed that employees, managers, and executives wanted and needed to change the way they were relating to each other.

For example, the average score in our survey for the item "I have a trusted relationship at work" was 1.5, on a 1 to 5 scale, with 5 being "strongly agree." Eighty-five percent of respondents scored this item at 1 or 2. Few people had a trusted relationship in this organization.

On another survey item, "If I could change for the better one thing about my workplace, I would change _____," respondents were asked to fill in the blank with one of five choices: "trust," "my relationship with my supervisor," "my relationship with my coworkers," "my pay," and "my job." Seventy-six percent of people filled in the blank with either "my relationship with my supervisor" or "my relationship with my coworkers." On every item pertaining to trust and relationship, the data showed in a convincing way that people within this organization wanted to improve their relationships with their supervisor and their coworkers—if only they knew how.

We were encouraged by our research—and intrigued. We were happy to discover that people actually wanted to have good relationships. But we were curious as to why they were not making it happen. What were we missing? What were they doing or not doing that prevented them from having the healthy relationships they wanted?

Ever had one of those days when your cup of coffee spilled but not one sprinkle got on your clothes? Or your toast fell out of your hand and landed with the jelly side up? Or your car ran out of gas just as you pulled into the gas station? No? Me either, but wouldn't it be nice if that happened just once? Something just as good happened for us as we were working with this organization.

The data, as I mentioned, revealed people wanted change in their relationships but did not know how to make change happen. We translated that to mean it was our task to make relationships happen. However, we could not make relationships happen for them. The employees themselves had to be the ones figuring out how to make relationships happen. Our task, as we eventually determined, was just to create opportunities for people to work on their relationships.

Once we laid out our modified strategy, the Board agreed with our plan. Tom and his team, however, were petrified. They were terrified of losing control. They felt our plan would confuse roles, dilute responsibility, undermine authority, and break up established teams. They were right. Our plan *deliberately* put existing roles, responsibilities, authority, and relationships into flux.

Once things got underway, however, Tom and his team recovered from their initial shock and even began to help us implement our ideas.

"What changed your mind?" I had to ask Tom.

"My team and I have struggled for three years to find a way to stop the fighting. But, instead of bringing a solution, we became part of the problem." Tom ran his fingers through his hair. "The Board has made it clear that this is our only chance to turn things around here. So we considered the options and concluded we have nothing to lose and everything to gain if what you recommend works to improve relationships. You can count on me and the executive team, as we have every intention of doing our part to help."

This was a Relationship-Impacting Opportunity, and Tom scored big! In that moment, by this act of humility, our appreciation for Tom and his leadership increased a hundredfold. Tom and his executive team made the choice to work on relationships.

Remember the coffee, toast, and gas serendipity? This was that kind of moment. The coffee spilled everywhere else but on us, the toast fell right side up, and the car ran out of gas right at the gas pump.

Tom said they had "every intention" to help. That word, *intention*, was like a flash of lightning, illuminating the sky. It was a simultaneous realization as everyone on our own team got the same idea at the same time.

"Intention, as in intentionality," we said in chorus.

Our team had already developed and delivered for other clients a program entitled "Intentionality: A Strengths-Based Approach to Performance." We designed the program to help people intentionally retain and apply concepts from Gallup's Strengthfinders, the Myers-Briggs Personality Type Indicator, and other such tools. We had found in our work that although people loved discovering their talent themes and their personality types, within ninety days most people were not using the information they had been taught. To overcome this lack of sustainability, we developed the intentionality program to help people become more intentional in using their strengths when doing daily tasks. Through this program, once people discover their personality types, strengths, or talents, we teach them about intentionality.

We use intentionality (as defined by Oxford Dictionary) as being deliberate or purposeful—directing your thoughts, beliefs, desires, and hopes toward some object or state of affairs.[4] We also use intentionality (as defined by Merriam-Webster Dictionary) as something that is done in a way that is planned or intended.[5] More simply put, we view intentionality as focusing and exerting effort upon accomplishing an outcome. In this way, we have seen outcomes such as job satisfaction, job performance, and the right job fit measurably increase as we teach employees how to become more intentional with their personality traits.

We knew about the power of intentionality as we started the work with Tom and his team. However, we struggled and wrestled for months with how to bring about change in this organization. It was Tom, of all people, who reminded us of this key idea: we choose how we behave—according to what we intend to achieve. If I intend to build more muscle, I go to the gym regularly, lift weights, and increase my protein intake—I adjust my behavior in order to get the results I want. If I intend to be considered for a role that requires specialized training, I enroll in the appropriate class—I change my behavior to increase my chances of getting the job.

Likewise, in relationships, we need to know what it is we intend to achieve and then change our behavior to match. In your relationships at home and at work, what is your goal, what do you hope to achieve, and how does your behavior align? This inquiry, captured in the one question "What is your intention?" was the impetus Tom and his people needed to ignite positive and pervasive change within their organization.

Intentionality, or choice, is a factor that is often overlooked in relationships, particularly those of family members. But it affects every interaction with spouses, siblings, and friends.

Look back to the quotes of husband and wife at the beginning of the chapter. It is easy to see that each had made a decision about the other. She decided he does not care. He decided she is a complainer. The result is that two people negatively impact their relationship by what they are doing or not doing for each other.

Too often, we do not see our relationships as resulting from what we do for and with each other. Instead, we tend to see many relationships as unplanned, naturally occurring, dynamic, haphazard events. Our society, elders, and experience reinforce this idea—that relationships, especially the best ones, "just happen."

How often have you said or heard the following statements of how relationships developed: "We bumped into each other at the food store, and things just developed from there"; "We met by chance"; "We kind of clicked together right away"; "We just seemed to like one another from the moment we met"; or "I knew right away we were going to be friends."

Or on the other hand, you may have heard or said, "My spirit did not take to him from the very first moment." "She has always rubbed me the wrong way." "Our personalities just clash all the time." In one view, relationships are often seen as out-of-body, beyond-our-control happenstances.

We tend to see relationships, especially the best ones, as something that happens naturally rather than a choice we make. Do not get me wrong; chance meetings, unplanned interactions, and divine interventions do happen. However, when relationships result from such events, their existence is driven by what both parties choose to do going forward. It is because of what you do—how each person uses self and what we choose to do with the opportunities presented—that relationships succeed or fail. But we have found that most people do not fully own or recognize the impact of their behavior upon relationships.

What you do in your relationships is always a choice. You actually choose how you behave in relationships. This is true in every setting—at home, at work, or in life in general. Even in instances where people are related to you by blood, you can and do choose whether or not you will have or maintain a relationship with them. You alone determine your relationships. You set the depth, length, and pace of your relationships. You decide when they come into existence, continue to exist, or become extinct. You hold the power over your relationships in your hands. You choose the persons with whom you spend time. You choose which persons at work or in social settings you get to know well or not at all.

So answer this: why are you in relationships with the people in your life? View the faces of family, friends, and coworkers as they flash before your eyes, stop on each one, and answer that question—why am I in relationship with him or her? I hope you answer that it is because you still choose to be in relationship with them.

Remember my friend Jack from the last chapter—he had an "aha" moment while he and I were on the phone as he was cooking for his wife? He realized that how you decide to do you is optional—and it is. He also realized that the choices he made in the past impacted his relationship success—and they do, all the time.

So what level of relationship success are you having? That is, how successful are you at relationships? Specifically, as a spouse, what choices are you making about how you do you in your relationship? As a parent, how are you doing you in your relationships with your children? As a brother or sister, how are you doing you in your relationship with your siblings? As a manager, how are you choosing to behave in your relationships with your employees? As an employee, how are you doing you in your relationship with your manager? As a coworker, how are you deciding to do you with your team members?

If your success isn't stellar, take some intentional action. Make the choice, like Tom, to take advantage of RIOs in your relationships.

I think my boss respects the work my team and I have done, especially with this latest assignment. We kicked butts to get this done on time and with efficient use of taxpayer dollars. We exceeded expectations. There were times when I needed to put the fire under people to get things done right and on time, but that is all part of the job. I get things done; nobody can deny that. I am not concerned if people like me. It is not my intention to win a popularity show. I am here to execute. If along the way some people get upset, well, maybe that's good; it means they care enough about the work. For me, that's mission accomplished.

—JOE

Joe really is brilliant. He has delivered every assignment with precision and beyond our expectations. But he is a bull in a china shop. He hurts and destroys morale. He intimidates people, and he discounts their opinions. Our leadership team is torn over what to do with him. We have intentions to promote him; I am retiring in a few months, and he has the vision and drive we need for our future. But, at present, there is just too much ill will toward him. His team, his peers, his customers, and my peers are at odds with him and his behavior. I just wish he would be good to people instead of pissing people off.

—JOE'S BOSS

CHAPTER FOUR

NOBLE YOU: BEING THE GOOD YOU IN RELATIONSHIPS

RELATIONSHIP IS INTENTIONALLY DOING GOOD.

The question "What is your intention?" became the clarifying and expectation-setting mantra for Tom, his team, and the entire organization. Tom's offer to help, and the epiphany that came with his response, moved our team to engage the leadership team in helping to rebuild relationships within the organization. And, to their credit, Tom and his organization consistently partnered with us to do the hard work that was required to change relationships. To start, they encouraged employees to examine their intention toward each other.

This was significant, as too often we are not mindful of how our behavior may be out of alignment with our original intentions.

We do not set out to build backstabbing, double-talking, or trust-busting relationships. The people at Tom's company had not. Most admitted that they did not plan to have unhealthy relationships. But, regrettably, somehow over the years, their behavior became less and less in sync with what they intended or expected from themselves or from others at work. Employees described that due to the cliquish way relationships worked within that organization, people felt forced to act in ways contrary to their own beliefs in order to belong. They confessed how they had compromised their own personal standards and had settled for subpar relationships.

This widespread admission was for Tom, for his team, and for us eye opening. We were surprised to learn that employees were heartbroken over lost or strained relationships. They poured out their feelings, some even crying during the interviews, owning their part in the dysfunction. Unanimously in the one-on-one sessions, people vowed to do whatever they could do personally to bring about change at an organizational level. We could hardly believe what was happening—Tom's people were actually yearning for a kinder, gentler workplace!

We had not seen this happen in this wholesale way in a company before—often with individual workgroups, couples, and families but not collectively from every employee, manager, and executive. People in this company started intentionally doing good!

People do not normally think of relationship in this way—as intentionally doing good. I do. I believe relationship flourishes when we take action that is intentionally uplifting. Parents, spouses, siblings, supervisors, and friends will benefit by asking the question "What is your intention?" as a way to point out good behavior that needs to be practiced in order to achieve the outcomes we want from our relationships. As it was, "What is your intention?" became a vital and compelling question in Tom's organization, so much so that people began asking for tools and strategies to help them repair broken relationships.

The first tool we gave them was a brief assessment called "Your Behavior/Intention Inventory." The inventory consisted of just five questions:

1. What relationship is foremost in your mind right now? Why?

2. What was your intention when you started your relationship with _____?

3. How does your behavior today align with your original intention for your relationship?

4. What behavior do you want to be known for in your relationship?

5. What behavior do you need to change in order to enhance your relationship? Why?

Take inventory of your relationships using these five questions to figure out where you need to become more intentionally uplifting. For Tom and his organization, this focus on "What is your intention?" was a rallying cry and a unifying event that got people focused upon intentionally doing good for one another.

Becoming intentional in a positive way, instead of the negative ways they had in the past, made a significant impact upon changing relationships for the better between Tom, his leadership team, and their employees. Dr. Renee Taylor, in her research, made a similar discovery: that becoming positively intentional can have a positive impact upon patients. As a result, she created what she calls the Intentional Relationship Model (IRM) to help occupational therapists improve their effectiveness with patients. Her work is centered on how therapists may, by being intentional, enhance their relationships with patients, shown in improved results. An article she wrote along with others explains the goals and use of her model:

> There are several goals related to the use of this model: First, therapists should use it as a tool for self-reflection to be able to shape and develop their relationship with clients intentionally.... The ultimate goal of IRM is to help therapists improve their relationships with clients, as this can help them provide their assistance to clients more effectively.[6]

Being intentional in relationships is a choice, one occupational therapists are making in order to help their patients. Think for just a moment about how relationships worked in your family while you were growing up. How did your parents do relationship with each other? How were they intentional with each other? With you and your siblings? How is your experience in your family impacting how you are intentional in your other relationships?

Relationships begin before we are born. From the very first kick or flutter in the stomach, mothers, doctors say, begin to form attachment to their babies.[7] As newborn babies, we have already had an average of forty weeks of pregnancy during which most mothers connect with their babies. Then, according to Mary Beth Steinfeld, MD, of University of California Davis Medical Center, it takes just days after birth before babies start reaching out to bond with their mothers:

A normal, full-term baby is . . . programmed to initiate and enter into a bonding relationship. Crying and
making other noises, smiling, searching for the breast,
and seeking eye contact gives cues for a caring adult to
respond. When a caregiver consistently responds to an
infant's needs, a trusting relationship and lifelong attachment develops.[8]

Since relationships are such an early and natural part of life,
why are we so often inept at forging and maintaining healthy
ones—both in the workplace and at home? We believe relationships require intentionality. By that, we mean that even the most
natural ones, like those between mother and child, still require
purposeful and determined action on the part of those involved.
We have to be intentional, in a good way, for any type of relationship to work. As intrinsic as the mother-child relationship is, it
still requires effort from both in order for bonding to occur.

Relationships do not just happen; as I've mentioned several times, we make them happen. Each one is made to happen
through a series of RIOs. This is what Tom and his employees
learned to use and use well. They learned to become intentional
in a positive way in their relationships. Relationship is having a
connection with or building a connection with another person.
However, the kind of relationship Tom and his organization
came to experience and enjoy defied and exceeded that definition.

They became more purposeful and determined in the way
they began to work and live together. For example, Kathy and
Donna, both of whom had decades at the company, were known
to be sworn enemies. They were notorious for delaying products
and services just because one did not want the other to succeed.
Then, after a training on intentionality, the two managers sent out

a joint email announcing that going forward, they would be intentionally positive in their relationship by meeting once a week at lunchtime to discuss ways to help each other serve the organization more effectively. Not long after that, the staff on both of their two teams was also interacting in a positive way.

In multiple ways across the organization, people were becoming more intentional in positively impacting relationships. What they were demonstrating is what we define as intentional relationships. To remind you, an intentional relationship is the *uplifting use of personality, conversation, insight, opinion, and influence to create and maintain a mutual and selfless connection with another person.*

This fully describes what we observed happening in Tom's workplace. He and his employees became interested in doing more of what was uplifting for the other person. They began to put to use self and that of others in an intentional way. They used conversation as an exchange of thoughts, ideas, and information with collaborative and mutually productive intent. They freely used their insight about themselves, their work, and the culture to help others. They gave and accepted permission to express opinions. They used their influence within the organization and outside to help coworkers succeed. And they did this all for the benefit of the mission of the organization and for the success of their colleagues.

Let's look at this idea in a different way. In the old days (my dating days were in the last century), prior to going out on yet another date—especially if there had been a series of dates—it was customary for the young man to be invited into the house of his date to answer one question from the parent: *What is your intention?* By this question, the parent was asking for the long range intentions the boy had concerning the relationship. In essence, they were saying: *Clarify for me what you intend to do with my daughter. Are you serious about her or just playing?* The parent was, by asking the question, giving a distinct message and setting the expected practice for dating that leads to marriage.

Most often, this was an embarrassing experience for the girl and an intimidating one for the boy. Yet for many couples, the memory of this event is a nostalgic one for them—a relationship-impacting one.

In this way, intention is an indicator of possible behavior. Our intention hints at what we may do, with whom we may do it, and, among other things, what desired result we may achieve by what we do. Modern-day retailers know this and count on understanding their customers' intention. Customer or buyer intention is a crucial part of retailers' strategy today. Retailers such as Hertz, Walmart, Nordstrom, and Toyota are all interested in understanding and assessing buyer intentions. Various methods, including surveys, free samples, interviews, and other market-testing activities, are used to assess buyer intention. Regardless of who the retailer is or what methods are used, they are all after one thing—how to influence people's behavior toward their product. The basic assumption is that intention has some relationship to behavior. It does.

Intention is a noun—it is a thought or idea. The verb form of intention is *to be intentional* and means to take purposeful action, to behave with specific intent. The behaviors impacting the relationships in Tom's organization were intentional. People were *mis*behaving intentionally. They were intentionally not returning phone calls. They were intentionally not forwarding helpful information to other teams. They were intentionally saying negative things about each other. They were intentional about doing things that hurt others and intentional about not doing things that would help others. Fortunately, over time, Tom and his employees came to realize the negative impact their intentional behavior was having on relationships.

Think about a specific relationship. What intentional behavior are you practicing in it at this time? In your career, what do you intend to achieve? How is your behavior impacting the relationships that can help you achieve your career goals?

What about your personal relationships? What do you intend to achieve? Are your behaviors aligned with achieving the harmony, respect, or love you intend? Usually, we start with good intentions at the beginning of a new relationship. Then, according to how the relationship is impacted by what we do or what the other person does, our intentions too often change for the worse.

This is sad—even tragic—not because it happens but because most times we can prevent this downward spiral by becoming more intentional in doing good. You may be saying, *I can accept the assignment of trying to intentionally do good, creating win-win events, but how do I, in a practical way, turn my existing relationships (some of which are great already, and others not so great, still others just bad and unhealthy) into intentional relationships? Is there a step-by-step process? One that I can easily learn and do?*

Stop right now and recall what your intentions were when you initiated a relationship. Write them down.

Do you still have those same intentions? What are your new intentions? Write those down.

What can you do today to intentionally score a RIO and improve your relationship? Write it down.

And do it.

In my practice, my foremost concern is caring for and connecting with my patients. Of course, technical expertise and precision are equally important. So when a patient showed me the mark on his stomach, I was dumbfounded. The mark was not there before the operation, and nothing happened during the procedure that would have caused it. I could tell that he was concerned about it, and I assured him I shared his concern. I could see it was not a rash or bruise; it was more like a birthmark. I admitted to him that I did not have a diagnosis or a remedy to remove it. We ended our visit with some remedies for him to try.

—DOCTOR

My surgery went well. The pain afterward was minimal, and the recovery time was short. However, there was an unexplainable mark on my stomach near the site of surgery which was not there prior to surgery. So in the post-op meeting with the surgeon, I asked him about it. He had no clue how it got there or what had caused the dark brown, three-

centimeter-by-six-inch streak down the right side of my stomach.

My doctor is one of the good guys; I like him. He is very professional and caring. I feel like I know him and I trust him. Yes, this mystery mark on my stomach is an annoyance, and I wish it were not there. It happened during surgery, and I want to know the cause and how to get rid of it. But I do not fault him for it, nor can I imagine pursuing legal consul. Like I said, I like him. Plus my health is much improved since he operated on me.

—PATIENT

CHAPTER FIVE

UPLIFTING YOU: GIVING OF YOURSELF IN RELATIONSHIPS

Tom and his leadership team took on the challenge and agreed to do whatever it would take to bring about positive change in relationships within their organization. However, they faced a historical and cultural dilemma—relationships were hostile and combative. The years of animosity and distrust were entrenched and would not dissolve quickly or readily. Intention to hurt and harm one another was the general frame of mind. People expected to get bad behavior from each other. They did not mind limiting outcomes if it meant getting back at someone who had inflicted hurt upon them. This was the norm in this organization. Once hired onto a team, employees were instructed and guided on how to interact (in an unhealthy way) with other teams and supervisors.

So although Tom and his executive team of eight had committed early on in the process to change, there were still three hundred other employees who did not as yet have a reason or appetite for changing relationships.

How do you change the historical mindset of a group bent upon hurting each other? Our answer: give them a reason to stop hurting and start helping each other—and use that reason to teach them how to change relationships. Nuclear energy may be used to destroy lives or provide electricity for millions. In the same way, RIOs may be used to destroy or build relationships; it depends upon our response to them. In an intentional relationship, we choose to let RIOs trigger only one response, and that is the lifting up of the other person. Remember, an intentional relationship is defined as the *uplifting* use of personality, conversation, insight, opinion, and influence to create and maintain a mutual and selfless connection with another person.

We introduced eight behaviors that they could use to start tearing down traditions and building up relationships. With them, you can learn to identify RIOs as they come, capitalize on the opportunity, and connect with your coworker, spouse, child, or friend.

1. Uplift
2. Understand
3. Talk
4. Study
5. Share
6. Influence
7. Serve
8. Change

As Tom's company worked through each of these ongoing behaviors, they saw tremendous results. They saw the fulfillment of the same three promises I make to you as you adopt the behaviors into your life and relationships:

- *To enhance your existing relationships:* For each relationship that you already have and want to keep, this book will teach you how to enhance them.
- *To decide what to do with an uncertain relationship:* For relationships you are uncertain why you are in, this book will help you decide to continue or quit.
- *To know when to terminate an unwanted or unhealthy relationship:* For those persons with whom you realize you do not want to be in relationship, this book will show you how to end it.

BEHAVIOR #1: UPLIFT

RIO: EVALUATE THE QUALITY OF THE RELATIONSHIP BY HOW YOU REACT TO RIOS.

Remember the "What is your intention" question? Tom and his organization now had a shared and positive answer: "to be uplifting." That response became the mindset for how they responded to RIOs. This group had a new reason, a "why" that they applied, with which they became intentional. Whenever Relationship-Impacting Opportunities occurred, they behaved in a way to create a win-win situation for each person. This is Behavior #1; assess your relationship based upon the response to RIOs. In your relationship, are RIOs scored, forfeited, or ignored? Are you uplifting?

Tom and his crew discovered how to bring value to each other once they understood why they should turn Relationship-Impacting Opportunities into winning events for each person. "When people uplift one another," I write in my book *Intentional Conversations: How to Rethink Conversation and Transform Your Career*, "they are more likely to share concerns and innovative ideas freely when they feel empowered, when they feel validated and accepted."

This was the case for Tom and his team. They started scoring RIOs; they turned relationships within their company into a winning, uplifting experience. And as they changed, the employees realized that they were getting farther in their own goals. Zig Ziglar, renowned author and motivational speaker, used to teach, "You can have everything in life you want if you will just help enough other people get what they want."

This is what it means to begin to build an intentional relationship—it means looking at the results coming out of your relationship with a critical eye. What is the present value of your relationship with your supervisor to you? Would you say it is uplifting for you or for them?

Your answer matters to your organization. What happens with RIOs impacts how an organization functions. When executives are at odds with one another, the managers below them are left to struggle with which executive it is in their best interest to follow and which one to ignore. This is the type of situation that breeds negative responses to RIOs. In Tom's organization, executives had established loyalties to the extent that managers who reported to them did not feel safe enough to talk to the "opposing" executive or their employees. As a result, outcomes were delayed often because groups refused to meet with each other to hand off work within the set deadlines for each stage.

Relationship-Impacting Opportunities also impact individual function at work. When an individual's relationships (especially those at work) are in conflict, employee engagement and productivity suffers. Employee sick days reach an all-time high. The human resources staff is bombarded with hostile work environment complaints. Relationships hit an all-time low until the individual begins to shift the focus from self to mission, from "me" to "us," and from "my team" to "our team." This is what happened in Tom's organization. They started learning how to apply their "why"—lifting each other up—instead of what they did in the past—stepping on others and pushing them down.

Mark and John, in Tom's company, had a lot to change when they began practicing the first of the eight behaviors. These two were on the same team. However, Mark was a manager and John was the union representative. Sparks flew often but in particular when either one tried to exert authority over the other. That is until one day when Mark made the first move toward John. He walked up to John and asked him if they could start afresh. John was reluctant, thinking that Mark had some ulterior purpose. It was not until one of Mark's employees had a labor-related incident that things changed.

In the past, Mark held firm on his position any time an employee called on the union to intervene in a dispute within his department. One way his resistance was conspicuous was in how he delayed the time of discussion to the maximum time allowed by the law. Delay was a well-known manager strategy to frustrate union representatives. That was until Mark came face to face with Behavior #1. Once he assessed his relationships, he realized that he was forfeiting important opportunities that he could be using to build relationships instead of breaking them down. Capitalizing on this RIO, he met with John and committed to expediting the schedule and working with him more agreeably.

Intentional relationships, like that of Mark and John, are more than just agreements between parties. It does not matter if it is in the workplace or at home; intentional relationships are covenants between people to be uplifting to each other. I use the word *covenant* here because it really is the only word that articulates the level of commitment required to establish an intentional relationship. It is also used because intentional relationships are more than giving and receiving. Intentional relationships are about giving yourself away—sacrificing in some way for the uplifting of the other person.

In this way, relationships are never equal—sometimes one person and sometimes the other is freely giving or freely receiving more. That is the true assessment. Are both parties in your relationship willing to accept the shared responsibility of building an uplifting relationship?

The results of intentionally uplifting those around you are far reaching. Look back to the quotes at the beginning of the chapter. Because the doctor established a healthy, uplifting relationship with his patient, he defused the threat of legal action for an uncertain side effect. The trust that was fostered because of the doctor's intention to uplift and to heal protected his own interests and maintained a healthy relationship.

Connecting with others, be it doctor with patient, husband with wife, parent with child, or manager with employee, has its own built-in rewards for all. We tend to know this—but how to intentionally connect with that one person is what most people want to know. Of course, connecting with persons whom you find difficult to connect with only concerns you if it is a relationship that you feel you want or must have for some reason. Examples of such relationships would be those we have due to family ties, maybe a child who has become estranged from you, a sibling with whom you have never gotten along, or an inherited in-law. Or perhaps it is a mandated work relationship such as with a supervisor or team member.

How can you make the most out of RIOs in your personal relationship, whether it is healthy, strained, or estranged? The next time you are about to spend time with a spouse, parent, sibling, supervisor, employee, or friend, assess your relationship by asking yourself these questions:

1. Do I know what my intention is in this relationship?

2. Am I willing to give myself away in order for this person to get what they want or need?

3. Am I willing to change my behavior to ensure that this is an uplifting relationship?

If you are able to answer yes to the questions above, this is a relationship that you want and need. Preserve and protect it.

A few months after I took over as the director of food services, one of my top performing kitchen workers stopped me. Early on, I had recognized that this particular employee appeared to have the potential to take on more responsibility than she had been given up to that point by her previous directors. So I gradually started giving her various opportunities in order to assess where the best fit was for her. I was pleased when in each instance she shone. In fact, it seemed that with each new task I assigned her, she did the new task better than the one before. I was very pleased with her. So when she stopped me and said, "Thank you, Miss Heather, for helping me," I immediately replied, "No, thank you. Thank you for being so very good at your job."

—MISS HEATHER, DIRECTOR

My reaction surprised Miss Heather. I broke down sobbing with body-shaking tears. She pulled me quickly into the office there at the back of the kitchen. She asked me to tell her why I was crying. I told

her how just prior to her coming to work in the caf-
eteria, I had concluded that my life was not worth
living anymore. I had made up my mind to end my
life. I had been busy putting things in order and
making plans for my suicide. However, once Miss
Heather started calling upon me at work, I began
to reconsider. I began to wonder if maybe there was
some reason to live after all.

"I just want to thank you for saving my life," I
told her. "Miss Heather, you just don't know how
much you mean to me."

—EMPLOYEE

CHAPTER SIX

UNIQUE YOU: ADDING YOUR PERSONALITY IN RELATIONSHIPS

I n Tom's organization, people were clueless about the workings of their own personality and knew even less about others'. As such, many opportunities for employees to work and succeed together were missed. Had the employee from the quote at the beginning of the chapter been a part of Tom's company, lacking the uplifting influence of Miss Heather's personality, she probably wouldn't have found her own strength and purpose.

However, as we progressed in our work in Tom's company, we began teaching them that an intentional relationship requires the uplifting *use of personality.*

Our personalities are revealed—what we are really like is exposed—in every relationship. As such, relationships highlight various parts of our personalities. The truth is that we are different people when we are with certain people. Every relationship has its own look and feel.

People in Tom's organization came to understand and manage the impact of relationship dynamics. Tom, against the grain of his natural inclination, was an example of how to intentionally use personality to change the dynamics of a relationship. To make the change, first Tom and the rest of the staff had to come to know their own personality as well as foster an understanding of the other people in their relationships.

BEHAVIOR #2: UNDERSTAND

RIO: RENOVATE OLD THINKING, ABOUT THEM AND YOU

An intentional relationship requires more than just knowing about a person—their name, height, weight, gender—it demands knowing a person. It asks you to discover what drives their behavior, their likes and dislikes, the experiences that have formed their thinking, etc. To develop an intentional relationship actually requires understanding personality, yours and that of others.

Remember, RIOs happen during each day. When they occur, people draw conclusions about who we are. They assess who we are through our behavior. It may be a simple behavior that was regular and very important, such as taking a message for a co-worker who is away from his or her desk and delivering it, or not, to them upon their return. Or as crucial as taking the time, even though busy, to be gracious in a way that prevents a suicide as in the story of Miss Heather and her employee. RIOs expose how we act and react, and people use that information to conclude whether we are caring or callous. Are we careful or careless? Are we a doer, thinker, or feeler? And so on. When RIOs expose our personality, we also invite our coworker or friend to bring to light parts of their own personality.

What is brought out when we interact within a given relationship is how we come to know that relationship. Ideally, all of our relationships would bring out the best in us all the time. It's not so. Relationships, in an indiscriminate way, reveal the good, bad, and ugly of who we are. Some of them bring out mostly the good in us, others a healthy mixture, while still others provoke the worst in us. In this way, each relationship has its own personality—its own dynamics. The one with your spouse, with your children, supervisor, or coworkers; each is a one-of-a-kind entity. They reveal and display different facets to the other person.

Although personality is at play in every interaction with another person, an interpretation of who a person is based only upon behavior is incomplete. Many of the problems in relationships are due to a lack of understanding the person beyond the behavior. In fact, a bigger part of the problem in most relationships is that most people do not understand their own personality and how it drives their behavior.

It was a major shift to change the culture at Tom's company to be one where supervisors, coworkers, and teams used an understanding of personality to uplift. To begin with, we did two things to expose how personalities were impacting behavior in their relationships. The first was to create a Project-Based Learning environment within teams. The second was to teach the whole staff how to identify, put to use, and manage their personalities.

Project-Based Learning (PBL) is an emerging instructional approach that school systems around the United States are beginning to adopt as a means to help students increase and develop problem-solving skills. Peggy A. Ertmer and Krista D. Simons of Purdue University in their article "Scaffolding Teachers' Efforts to Implement Problem-Based Learning" state:

> Research suggests that effective use of problem-based learning methods can prepare students to be flexible thinkers who can work productively with others to solve problems. Moreover, the PBL method has been demonstrated to increase different types of problem-solving skills in students, from describing specific processes needed to address a particular problem, to increasing the depth and breadth of solutions.[9]

We use PBL for exactly the same purpose—plus one. We use PBL to observe personalities. The various personalities in a group emerge revealingly as people work on assigned tasks. To observe and teach how personality impacted relationships as managers and employees worked in newly assigned teams, we identified a real-life, real-time project. We assigned employees and managers the task to define why and how they would do specific procedures differently in order to help another team get projects done more easily, quickly, or cost effectively.

We were worried that the level of effort would be seen by employees, especially those who were not used to having the power to change things, as too difficult or threatening. Instead of us assigning individuals to tasks, we had employees select and form working groups with those outside of their normal teams to brainstorm and develop ideas. They rose to the task and provided logical and practical reasons for the changes they would make. And they also provided the process by which those changes could be implemented. To ensure the least disruption of processes and service, work assignments and reporting structures were changed.

Changing tasks and supervision thus also required a change in roles and responsibilities. So, with the Board's continued support, we had workgroups change roles and responsibilities to ensure that the changes got done. Finally, we advised the Board that authority would also have to change in order to allow decisions to be made readily at the point of contact by the most informed persons. Once again, they agreed. Front-line supervisors and managers immediately began making decisions that changed team membership. As team membership changed, new alliances and relationships began to form, happily, without the negative behavior of the past. And, equally important, they included an additional ingredient—intentional use of personality. Educating the staff about personality and the significant part it plays in interaction was the second part of our training.

What does personality at work look like? One aspect of personality is the ability to recognize RIOs and the attitude toward capitalizing on them. In the company, there were those people whose personality drove them to be constantly looking for ways to connect with others. When an opportunity to enhance their relationship with someone occurs, these folks recognize it right away. They know exactly how to make the most of the opportunity.

Other personality types, also present in this organization, were less likely to be aware of when a Relationship-Impacting Opportunity has occurred. They missed them completely, finding out later only when and if someone informs them.

Then there were those who had the personality to create Relationship-Impacting Opportunities. They actually plan them beforehand and then execute them with precision.

Regardless of what personality type you are, RIOs are occurring within your reach, and it is to your benefit to put them to good use. Tom, for example, was not the type to notice when a

RIO occurred or to create one when they did not. No one would ever accuse him of being "touchy-feely," and he liked it that way. So imagine the personal crisis we created for Tom as we began teaching that relationship and organizational success are directly connected to how a leader responds to and acts upon RIOs. Tom was in a quandary—he desperately wanted to succeed, but if success depended upon him becoming who he was not, he was doomed to failure.

You may have a personality similar to Tom's, and this discussion is causing you unease. No worries; people with all types of personality face and overcome the challenge of learning how to use their unique difference, their personality, in an effective way in relationships.

For everyone, regardless of personality type, daily interactions at home and at work present Relationship-Impacting Opportunities through which we can change, enhance, and preserve relationships. Everyone needs to become proficient in putting them to use.

To get the most out of RIOs by using your personality, you must first know and understand the characteristics of your personality. And one recommendation I give when training on understanding personality is to seek out a relationship assistant.

Gary and Betsy Ricucci, in their book *Love That Lasts*, in describing the marriage relationship, put it this way:

> One of the best wedding gifts God gave you was a full-length mirror called your spouse. Had there been a card attached, it would have said, "Here's to helping you discover what you're really like!"[10]

Marriage provides us with one full-length mirror—our spouses; work provides us with many more—our managers, employees, and coworkers. Through their reflection to you, and yours to them, there are multiple opportunities each day that reveal who we are. What are you seeing? Do you like what you see?

At the beginning, Tom and his employees did not like what they saw, and they decided to use their personalities to do something about it. Here's what they did:

- They learned to appreciate and celebrate personality types
- They learned to talk plainly about personality types
- They learned to use personality to increase performance

THEY LEARNED TO APPRECIATE AND CELEBRATE PERSONALITY TYPES

Alan Chapman in his article "Personality Theories, Types, and Tests" explains the value that comes from a knowledge of personality types:

> Developing understanding of personality typology, personality traits, thinking styles and learning styles theories is also a very useful way to improve your knowledge of motivation and behaviour of self and others, in the workplace and beyond. Understanding personality types is helpful for appreciating that while people are different, everyone has a value, and special strengths and qualities, and that everyone should be treated with care and respect.[11]

Through trainings on personality, all three hundred employees were taught how to unleash and appreciate their personality and that of their coworkers. Tom and his deputy Brad, for example, were surprised to discover that Tom's appetite for trailblazing and Brad's appetite for caution, which often caused conflict once they began to develop an intentional relationship, was actually of benefit to them. When they learned how to put their very different, in some ways opposite, personalities to use, they found that they actually came up with complementary viewpoints, which resulted in more effective solutions.

Can you see the differences in your spouse and appreciate how his or her difference makes you a better team?

THEY LEARNED TO TALK PLAINLY ABOUT PERSONALITY TYPES

Once these folks began to understand themselves, there was no keeping them quiet. Employees and managers alike were spontaneously sharing with one another their results. Amazingly, they explained both how their tendencies work for them and how they worked against them. A new level of trust and transparency emerged—and RIOS were bringing positive and transformative results.

Can you talk to your friends with openness and trust about how your tendencies work for the benefit of your friendship?

THEY LEARNED TO USE PERSONALITY TO INCREASE PERFORMANCE

Early in our assignment with Tom and his team, we tried to have team-building sessions. They failed miserably, people had meltdowns, and the meetings quickly spiraled down to such a degree we had to stop holding the meetings. But once people understood how to use their personalities in an intentional way, the exact opposite started happening. Managers and teams volunteered themselves and each other for tasks and roles.

Michelle, for example, always felt that people did not really like her because she was known as a no-nonsense and "this is what the rules say" type of person. Yes, people respected and deferred to her, she told us, but they really did not care to be in the same space with her. However, once she understood how her personality brought a unique viewpoint to bear, and that people actually valued it, she volunteered to become the union representative "to ensure that employees and the organization reach the goals we set," she said.

Can you utilize the very traits that make you you to improve your work life? Your home life? Your social life?

The degree of success you experience, Tom and his people were learning, is directly connected to how you use your personality to relate to one another.

In my book *Intentional Difference: The One Word That Changes Everything*, we identified three zones of performance that can be achieved according to how you use your personality or, as we describe it in the book, how intentional you are with your difference.

The first zone is the Distraction Zone. This is where you have not yet discovered how to fully use your personality. In this zone, the vast majority—roughly 85 percent—of what you are capable of doing most anyone can do. Think about it: are you really the only one, or even the only one in your company, who can host a meeting? Who can crunch the numbers? Or even write up a problematic situation so that it sounds like an exciting challenge rather than a dreaded duty? These are the tasks that appear urgent but are, in fact, not utilizing our unique personality—anybody can do them.

The tragic fact is that most of us spend most of our time mired in the 85 percent where our unique personality makes very little difference. It's not that those things are not important. They may be part of your job description, and you may have to do them regularly in order to fulfill your role or to make your company function. But the skills to complete these tasks—no matter how necessary they may be—are not unique to you; they do not emerge from what makes you different.

As a result, these activities—these duties, if you will—do not elicit passion or full engagement from you. You may feel compelled to do these things, but the fact is there are others who naturally perform these activities with much greater effectiveness than you do.

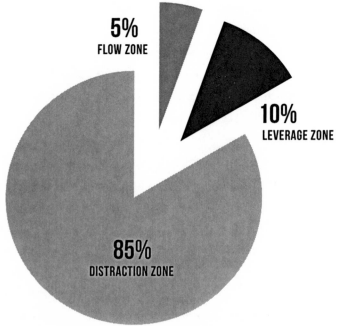

A much smaller percentage—say 10 percent—resides in the Leverage Zone. It consists of what you are capable of doing that select others can be trained and deployed to do. These include highly skilled tasks, maybe even tasks for which you have earned an advanced degree. Creating that job-specific spreadsheet, for example. Or even motivating the sales team to tackle a particularly challenging quarter. These activities may elicit a very high output from you. They may draw on your creativity, and you may perform them with excellence. However, you execute them based upon your technical knowledge or deep industry experience based on something you've learned—something you've been trained to do or trained yourself to do.

The fact is that there are others who could be trained to do them just as well. These tasks are not spontaneous for you. You have minimal passion when doing them. You do them when called upon to do so. These activities are still not hitting that sweet spot for you.

That 5 percent of what your personality equips you to do—the Flow Zone—is different. This 5 percent of what you are capable of doing only you can do—or only you can do in the way you do it. This 5 percent is the capacity from which you contribute uniquely; the invigorating well from which you draw when you are doing things at which you are remarkably, amazingly effective. This is the source from which you draw life and joy, the space where you are doing what only you can do. It's the special ingredient that adds incredible value to your professional and personal relationships.

The Flow Zone is you fully using your unique personality. Understanding your unique personality can help you begin using your personality to renovate or strengthen a relationship.

Tom and his executives shifted responsibilities and teams so that they could utilize the 5 percent Flow Zone to improve their company, their relationships, and their work satisfaction. As a result, they and many of their employees saw their true reflection for the first time in the full-length mirror of a manager, coworker, or friend in the office.

Do you have someone you can recruit as your relationship assistant? Give the person permission to be a full-length mirror to show you who you are. At home, is it your spouse, your parent, your adult child, or your best friend? At work, is it a colleague, a supervisor, an employee, or a mentor? Be sure they are someone who cares about you and knows you well.

Give them permission to reflect to you how your personality impacts others. Let them give you examples from the past and feedback as examples occur in the present. Then, as you are learning from them, you will find that you are developing an intentional relationship with them. After all, an intentional relationship is about understanding the "who"—who you are and who the other person is—so that you may be uplifting in your *use of personality.*

Co-pilot: "It's been a while since we've been de-iced."

Several minutes passed, as the pilot and co-pilot continued to remark on the difficult conditions, including ice build up on plane that had just landed.

Co-Pilot: "Look how the ice is just hanging on his back, back there, see that? Side there . . . See all those icicles on the back there and everything

Pilot: Yeah

More minutes pass.

Co-Pilot: "Boy, this is a losing battle here on trying to deice those things, it gives you a false feeling of security, that's all that does."

The plane was shortly cleared for takeoff. The plane moved down the runway and started to climb. The pilots immediately began to run into trouble

Co-pilot: "God, look at that thing (indicator)! That doesn't seem right, does it?"

Pilot: (silence)

Co-pilot: "Ah, that's not right."

Pilot: "Yes it is . . . there's eighty."

Co-pilot: "Naw, I don't think that's right . . . ah, maybe it is.

Pilot: Hundred and twenty

Co-pilot: "I don't know."

The stall warning began to sound. The plane stopped climbing and began falling back toward the ground.

Pilot: "Come on! Forward! Just barely climb." Five seconds pass.

Co-pilot: "Larry, we're going down! Larry—!"

Pilot: "I know it—!"

—AIR FLORIDA FLIGHT 90, JANUARY 13, 1982

CHAPTER SEVEN

CONVERSATIONAL YOU: ACTIVELY ENGAGING IN RELATIONSHIPS

The type of relationships Tom and his employees had at work was directly related to the frequency and quality of the conversations managers were having with their employees and conversations employees were having with other employees. In those old, negative instances, inappropriate conversations damaged relationships, such as when words were used to intimidate, harass, or exclude employees from a clique. But as the company culture changed, there were more positive instances, where conversations between employees reinforced the norms and expectations of the work culture, current goals, and ways to achieve them. Through conversations, relationships, casual and more personal, develop. And over time through repeated conversation, employees often experience trust, camaraderie, mutual respect, and team spirit.

If you look to the quote at the beginning of the chapter, you'll see an instance of failed communication. Those were the last words on the cockpit voice recorder. As the plane crashed into the Potomac, it killed the pilot, copilot, and seventy-six passengers; four people were killed in their cars on the 14th Street Bridge.

Had the pilot acknowledged and acted on the communication of his copilot, they could have serviced the plane and avoided the accident entirely.

Our definition of an intentional relationship is the uplifting use of personality, conversation, insight, opinion, and influence to create and maintain a mutual and selfless connection with another person. The emphasis in this chapter upon the *use of conversation* takes on dire significance when we think of the role conversation played in the fateful Air Florida flight 90.

BEHAVIOR #3: TALK

RIO: PRECIPITATE BEHAVIOR CHANGE BY WHAT YOU SAY.

Conversation is the universal means by which people engage one another. Wherever humans live, conversation is present. Using different sounds, words, and symbols, humans conduct conversations in a variety of languages, in every culture, around the world. As compulsory as breathing is, so is the human need to engage in conversation. What we say in conversation matters. Through conversation, people decide whether they like us or not, whether to follow us or not. Through conversation, we define who we are, who we want to become, and what our value is to others. Most importantly, through conversation we prescribe what type of relationship we have and with whom.

Changing communication to uplift is often simple with a peer, a friend, or a coworker. However, there is often greater challenge in changing conversations between manager and employee. Managers tend to flounder when it comes to relationships, The Gallup Organization—a research-based, performance-management company—reports.[12] Their research reveals fifty percent of employees who voluntarily leave leave due to limited or poor communication with their manager. The fact is that few managers are having relationship-building conversations with their employees. This creates a sad, recurring cycle—managers do not have conversation with their employees, and as a result, most employees do not know how to have a conversation with their manager.

Tom's organization experienced this cycle even more dramatically due to the ongoing turf battles. Most conversations were done in a way to command and control others. However, this all changed once managers and employees began to learn how to use conversation in a way that optimized each Relationship-Impacting Opportunity. My team's job, then, was to teach them how to turn mere conversations into intentional conversations. An intentional conversation, as I write in *Intentional Conversations*, is "a spoken exchange of thoughts, ideas, and information with collaborative and mutually-productive intent."[13]

We taught Tom and his employees how to practice conversation using the SECRET process. These six letters (S-E-C-R-E-T) provide a mechanism by which you can become more intentional in how you use conversation to change behavior. The SECRET acronym teaches how to do six action steps:

Suspend Status is the first action step in SECRET. To "suspend status" means to own the status you have within a relationship but to choose to behave and communicate in a way that values and esteems the other person as equal to or higher than yourself.

Empower Others is the progressive next action step in the SECRET process—for managers, employees, husbands, wives, etc.—to change their conversation and relationship by empowering each other. Empower each person. To empower a person, in this context, is to be intent on serving the other person in a way that validates that you have their interests and well-being in mind.

Cultivate Connection is the third action step in SECRET. To cultivate connection is to make conversation about investing the time, energy, and risk needed to create an environment of mutual giving and receiving needed in order to forge a deeper relationship. Cultivating a connection is work for both parties. Where suspending status is work for a manager or anyone with status in the relationship and empowering each other is work for each individual, cultivating connection requires mutual effort on the part of both parties. If any party missteps here, the relationship will remain at a superficial conversation level.

Reframe Reaction means that we manage our reaction during the conversation in a way that ensures that the conversation progresses. Having an intentional conversation requires being mindful of both your needs and those of the other person. Intentional conversations happen within the context of a mutually beneficial exchange. Each person is intent on helping the other succeed, which is why the reframe reaction step is fourth in the progressive process of the SECRET formula. In steps one, two, and three, manager and employee have invested time, effort, and risk. Once both parties have participated in suspending status, empowering each person, and culti-vating connection, a mutual investment has been made. By step four, we are emotionally invested. We have "skin in the game," so to speak. We have given enough in ex-change during the previous three steps to be interested in a good return.

Enforce Engagement is the fifth action step that must be practiced in the SECRET process. Sounds a bit strong? Absolutely! At this stage in the conversation, you have paid your dues; you have done the hard work of sus-pending status, empowering others, cultivating connec-tion, and reframing reaction. You are at the place in the conversation where it is now appropriate that you assert (and insist) that your ideas, thoughts, and information are valued and acted upon.

This is a difficult and uncomfortable action step for many. But be encouraged: this step, once applied, can bring immediate and memorable results. This was the case for the passengers, including myself, on United Flight 3774 from Minneapolis to Washington Dulles.

Entering the plane a bit ahead of me, a passenger spoke to the flight attendant who was standing at the door. The passenger was concerned about the two inches of snow that had collected on the plane. Marieka, the flight atten-dant, responded by saying to the passenger, "He is stand-ing right behind you."

The passenger, not understanding her meaning, said, "That's okay, he can wait. I just want to know that this plane will be de-iced prior to takeoff." The man quietly standing just behind the passenger was actually Captain Jason Gray, who had just come back from his preflight check. Having overheard the conversation, he spoke up and assured the passenger, "I got it covered."

The man nodded and proceeded to his seat.

About fifteen minutes after we had been seated, Captain Gray made this announcement: "Folks, we are almost ready to depart. Before we depart, we will be de-icing the plane. This is the process: first you will see that they spray an orange-colored solution on the plane—this is to take the existing ice off the plane. Then they will apply the solution a second time—this is to keep the ice off the plane. You should actually smell the solution once the process gets started. Thank you for your concern, and we appreciate your trust. Your safety is our number one concern."

I was especially grateful for this experience for two reasons. First, I was grateful that Marieka and Captain Gray had accepted the challenge of having an intentional conversation. Second, I was especially grateful for the passenger who enforced engagement from others.

Let me explain. No doubt, the de-icing was already scheduled and was going to happen regardless of the passenger asking about it. But just the same, everybody on that plane benefited from the additional information and assurance that resulted from this intentional conversation. Through intentional conversation, we insist that critical and important issues get the focused attention and action that we desire. Captain Gray, Marieka, and the concerned passenger, through their brief but intentional exchange, identified, discussed, and acted upon an important, potentially life-threatening issue. In this example—and any time where there is an intentional conversation—the parties involved, as well as others, benefit from enforced engagement. Passengers on another flight, Air Florida Flight 90, from the excerpt at the beginning of this chapter, were not so fortunate. The conversation that ensued prior to their flight did not have the crucial enforce engagement step of an intentional conversation.

Triage Takeaways is the last action step in the SECRET process. Triage is a crucial and immediate action step during a medical emergency. It saves lives by sorting patients so that those with the most severe, life-threatening injuries get treatment first. Triage is every bit as serious and useful when it comes to conversation.

Conversation is a selective process. It is like a refiner's fire, a potter's lathe, and a farmer's threshing floor. The ideas, thoughts, and information presented during a conversation are instantly examined, tagged, and sorted by both parties. Some of the ideas, for example, get tagged in the "do not retain" group—these are discarded almost immediately. Other ideas are put into a "more conversation required" group—these may be discussed more right then or at a later time. Still other ideas are put into the "this is important, urgent, upsetting, and problematic" group, and from the moment they are uttered, they become the passionate or focused subject for the rest of the exchange.

At this point, we care how the conversation ends. That is why we insist that this sequence is so important in the SECRET process. We need the previous steps to be accomplished in order to move on to the next step. First, we let people know that we value them as equal and not beneath us (Suspend Status). Then we serve others instead of looking to be served (Empower Others). Once we have established level ground and created an atmosphere of mutual service to each other, we then give and receive permission to build a valuable relationship (Cultivate Connection). We get that permission only when we have moved from a superficial "us versus them" level to a more in-depth, reciprocal relationship. Once we start to go deeper, we become more reciprocal, which increases our desire for a mutually beneficial outcome from our conversation. To achieve the desired outcome, both parties now must be willing to monitor and modify their responses during the conversation to ensure there is continuous forward movement (Reframe Reaction).

By Enforcing Engagement, we ensure that our communication is valuable and worth action from the other person. While you might not need this particular step in every conversation, you do need the skill to be able to assert your position clearly and without unhealthy attempts to control others with your conversation. And with Triage Takeaways, you understand how to best compartmentalize and act on the Enforced Engagement of the person with whom you are conversing.

Every idea, thought, and bit of information shared during a conversation gets filed in some way based upon the next step the person has decided to take. In this way, conversation is the refining, forging, and interpreting of messages we give and receive from each other. In essence, during each conversation, we are creating something new out of what the other person presents, and we offer that back to the other person, who, in turn, does the same. This process can be a positive and productive cycle.[14]

Too often, however, it is not. Conversations spiral down. They deteriorate to the point where we lose the opportunity to take away new ideas, thoughts, and information from each other. This does not have to be the case; we can learn how to optimize every conversation by learning how to use conversation right—to build up, not break down, relationships.

Using conversation right, at the right time, can save lives and prevent problems. And using conversation right changes how we are experienced by others with whom we are in relationship. This is why the SECRET process is so important: each step safely progresses the conversation and, consequently, the relationship to a deeper and deeper level.

An intentional conversation taps into resources that each person brings and reveals them so that they may be put to use. It is like what a farmer does by tilling the soil—he frees up the nutrients by digging down below the encrusted earth to get to the fresh soil. The SECRET process helps us to break up the fallow ground in relationships—helps us remove the scar tissue of old and failing conversation behavior. It exposes and demonstrates our tenderness—the touchy-feely or open part of a healthy conversation that many people resist. Yielding and giving to another person is like that: it reveals our vulnerability. And it is vulnerability that is both the requirement and reward of an intentional conversation—for as we open our hands and hearts up to give, we are also opening them up to receive.

This type of conversation ushers a manager, employee, supervisor, subordinate, spouse, teacher, student—whomever—to a higher and deeper level of relationship. Each person begins to realize and own that he or she can have meaningful and mutually beneficial conversations and relationships by taking the risk to give and receive during an intentional conversation.

It was quite interesting to see the evolution of relationships in Tom's organization as people began applying these six steps to conversation in a way that created community. An intentional relationship is about how to turn RIOs, through the uplifting use of conversation, into relationship-building events—every time.

So how can you use SECRET with your spouse or your child to strengthen your relationship? How can you use conversation to reveal whether to continue or end a partnership or friendship? Start by doing the following:

1. *Listen* to what you say and how you say it in your relationships.
    - Are your words uplifting?
    - Do you care what impact the things you say are having upon the other person?
    - Do your conversations put you in the one-up or one-down position?

2. *Visualize* what it would be like not to have conversations with the person.
    - If you were not having regular conversations with this person, what would you be missing?

- Would they be missing anything if the conversations were to stop?
- Looking back over the time you have had in relationship with this person, what specific benefit can you identify that has resulted from your conversations?

Use the SECRET to conversation to find your voice and to strengthen your relationships. Make communication an uplifting experience for yourself and the people in the circle of your influence.

Looking back on who I was when we started in our relationship, I am amazed. We were so different, even opposite in many ways. He loved being in front of people, talking. I preferred to be in the background. It was not that I did not have ideas or insight that could have added to the discussion or conversation; I just did not feel the need to speak up often.

That is until I realized how my life experiences—my pain, my broken marriage, my loss of family, my story—can help other people. The first time I told my story, I was petrified. Then I was asked to tell it again and again. And people would come up to me with tears in their eyes, saying how I had given them hope by what I said. I realized quickly that many people were living my story as well. Recognizing that people needed to know that there is hope and healing after adultery, regardless if you are the hurting or hurtful partner—that is when I discovered my voice.

—WIFE

Watching her speak before a group is really an amazing sight. She speaks with such passion and caring that endears her to audiences quickly. When she speaks about my affair, her heartbreak, and our journey, she is fearless. People who knew her before are struck by the power and presence she has when she stands up to speak. The transformation in her is truly remarkable. She has chosen to turn her pain into profit for others.

—HUSBAND

CHAPTER EIGHT

INSPIRATIONAL YOU: PRACTICING INSIGHTFULNESS IN RELATIONSHIPS

Tom's organization was charged with providing services such as emergency personnel and equipment during major weather events. If there was a flood, snowstorm, or hurricane, Tom and his people were in the midst of it, helping to save lives. Yet in the days prior to the change that was now happening, the mission of rescuing people was oftentimes lost amidst the drama within this hostile work environment. Why? Because a "me" focus cancels out a mission focus every time. Don Clifton, mentor and friend, stressed, taught, and lived the concept of personal mission and purpose. In his book *Soar with Your Strengths*, he writes: "Mission gives purpose to life. It adds meaning to what one does. In its purest form, it is so deeply felt that it explains why one does what one does."[15]

As Tom gained insight into himself and others, he also got more clarity about the mission—his and that of the organization. Insight is the capacity to gain an accurate and deep intuitive understanding of a person or thing. To have an intentional relationship, as you may recall, requires the mutually uplifting *use of insight* to create and maintain a selfless connection with another person.

To gain insight, we need to look at the people around us, learn what makes them function the way that they do, and connect more strongly based on what we come to understand.

BEHAVIOR #4: STUDY

RIO: EDUCATE YOURSELF ABOUT THE PERSON'S STRENGTHS AND PERSONALITY.

Van Brown, a preacher friend of mine whom I find to be a very insightful person, sat with a group of men in his church and asked them, "What would you do differently if you had a chance to start all over again?" Each of them without hesitation identified specific and concrete examples of how they had failed to be the leader in some way, whether in their homes, in the church, or in life.

"I was surprised," Van said, "and disappointed to hear the sense of loss and resignation in their voices, especially since we were several weeks into my series teaching on the subject 'How to Walk in Your Greatness.' It seemed they had not grasped yet the core idea I had been teaching them—God has a purpose for your life now, in spite of your past. I was not ready to give up on them as yet, so I took action to ensure they got the message by asking another question.

"'What prevents you from accomplishing those goals now?' I asked them. For every excuse they gave me as to why they could not succeed, I challenged them with the question 'Is it too big for God Almighty to make a way for you to succeed?'

"For two hours we discussed, at times debating quietly, at other times shouting loudly; still at other times we sat in sullen silence. Until finally they got it—because I finally got it. They were not afraid to fail; they had done that most of their lives. They had prison records, alcoholism, and addictions in their past—for some of them it had been months, for some, years.

"But, for all of them, failure was not threatening; success was. Any success, such as keeping a job or remaining sober, meant they had to change their friendships, their living arrangements, and how they spent their free time. The thought of such upheaval in their lives was immobilizing. Once I got that, I was able to see how I could help them begin to succeed. I knew they got it once they started to brainstorm about how at least some version of each man's dreams was still realizable, in the present day. They got there finally—on their own, one by one. They got back from this discussion everything and more of what they put in when they realized it sometimes takes pain to gain."

One of the most helpful things you can do for a person is to really get to know them—to strive to know them. Study people. Gain insight into people—as Van did above—so that both of you get the most out of your efforts. Based upon the insight you gain, sometimes this will mean putting more effort into enhancing the relationship. Other times, it will mean putting more effort into terminating the relationship.

Every time a RIO occurs, we have the option to gain insight. However, only when we invest time and energy to study—that is, to gain insight into—another person are we able to be intentional in our relationship with that person. Like the husband from the quotes at the beginning of the chapter who came to see his wife in a new light and appreciate her strength, we can all change our relationships into intentional relationships by studying the other person.

To be intentional in their relationships, husbands and wives, parents and children, brothers and sisters, managers and employees, coworkers, and friends need to study one another to help each other grow and succeed.

Remember in Chapter Six when we wrote about how to use personality? In that chapter, we were talking about how to use personality to be uplifting. At the end of that chapter, we introduced the three zones of intentional difference. We identified the Distraction Zone (where you are mired in activities that are not part of your Intentional Difference, or ID, but are part of the 85 percent of what you are capable of doing that most anyone can do). And we talked about the Leverage Zone (or the 10 percent select others can be trained to do just as well as you). And lastly, when talking about your ID, we are specifically referring to your 5 percent, your Flow Zone.

"Flow" is not a new concept. Given a name by the psychologist Mihaly Csikszentmihalyi, flow describes that incredible experience where everything but the present moment falls away and you are totally and incredibly focused on excellence. And it's not trying to be excellent—you are excellent in what you do in this zone. We taught Tom and his managers about how to spend more time in their flow zone.

Using the principles I outlined in my book, *Intentional Difference*, we taught them to use the six dimensions of ID to understand themselves. Just as important, however, we also taught them how to use these dimensions of Intentional Difference to study and unleash their employees' performance:

- Critical Outcome
- Driving Passion
- Assimilated Experience
- Cumulative Knowledge
- Emergent Skill
- Prevailing Talent

CRITICAL OUTCOME

Use this dimension to reinforce or repair brand image. A brand is a set of behaviors that a person becomes known for. It describes what he or she successfully accomplishes over and over again. Marketing experts are paid millions of dollars to capture an individual's or company's essence in an image or slogan—in a brand. Your brand is the thing for which your friends and coworkers know they can count on you to do time and time again. In this way, your brand is valuable both to you and to others. Reinforce it. Recruit your family, friends, managers and coworkers; give them permission to study you, to get to know you well enough to help you use your 5 percent more to strengthen your brand. Know their Flow Zone. Offer the same support to them. Be on the lookout for opportunities to enrich and expand yours and the other person's Critical Outcome.

DRIVING PASSION

Use this dimension to clarify and cultivate the thing or things for which you have an intense, energizing appetite that demands action. It drives your behavior. You may get paid for this or you may not, but even if you are paid—you would do it for free. This is the thing that raises your heart rate, that makes the hair on the back of your neck stand up, that gives you chills, that makes you weep and pound the table or dance around the room. You cannot NOT do this thing. It drives you and you can't get enough of it.

As a manager or a spouse or a friend, you act on your passions, invite others to join you in it, or bless their lives by it. You watch and see what drives your employees or your spouse or your friend, and you encourage them to embrace that passion, give them liberty to explore it, and observe how their driving passion enlivens all of your experiences.

ASSIMILATED EXPERIENCE

Use this dimension to discover the historical perspective that shapes, informs, and directs your behavior. As we move through life, we are always accumulating experience—good and bad, triumphant and painful, lessons learned and disasters averted. All of those experiences shape us uniquely as they are assimilated into the fabric of our ID.

Watch for the experiences that build the people around you. Observe how your experiences shape the way you see others in your relationships. Then embrace the perspectives and experiences that strengthen you and prevent the negative experiences from clouding your judgment or interactions. Foster an increased compassion and grow added excitement.

CUMULATIVE KNOWLEDGE

Use this dimension to understand how you learn best. From our earliest days—even in the womb—we are learning. As we age, we are influenced by teachers, experiences, books we have read, courses we take, mentors who invest in us, and academic degrees we acquire. There is no limit to our capacity to learn and the places we can draw this knowledge from.

What makes this particular dimension part of your ID is that there are certain learning experiences that are "sticky"; they adhere to you and become part of who you are and what you do. Cumulative knowledge is your unique retention and purposeful use of information.

Use your understanding of your own cumulative knowledge, and that of those around you, to turn training and learning moments into RIOs.

EMERGENT SKILL

Use this dimension to isolate the skill where you have the most potential for greatness. All of us have things that we are just naturally good at doing, in many cases, remarkable things that just come easy to us. This innate ability—which we call "emergent skill"—is honed and shaped, but the important thing to understand about emergent skill is that we are born with it. It is our innate ability, our spontaneous behavior that finds automatic and repeated expression and so is part of our ID.

Cultivate your emergent skill. See if there are opportunities at home or at work to expand your ability. And, where possible, give others that same freedom. Like our Driving Passions, Emergent Skill opens doors for new, innovative solutions and blessings.

PREVAILING TALENT

Use this dimension to dig deeper into what lies behind your perspective, behavior, and appetite. You are unique. You think, feel, and behave like no one else does. You process information, experience emotion, solve problems, and communicate with others in ways that are all your own. You are so you! We call this sixth dimension Prevailing Talent, and it is your spontaneous, reliable, and measured pattern of thinking, feeling, and behaving. Take what insights you find in your Prevailing Talent, and use that understanding to do *you* better!

Using the six dimensions to understand others results in two things: an increased insight into the unique and useful difference each person brings with them and a shared insight into how to multiply the success of each person.

Understanding your Intentional Difference helps you want to make an intentional difference—it clarifies your life's mission. This was the case for Tom. As he became a student of how the six dimensions impacted behavior and outcomes, he made a pivotal discovery about himself. He discovered that he was unhappy and angry most of the time—mainly because his job was no longer aligned with his mission. This led to a love-hate relationship with the Board and his executive team. As a result, his response in most relationship-impacting situations with them was negative. His frustrated state made him not care enough to want to score on RIOs. He finally admitted to himself that he hated his job.

People are made different to make a difference—it is an innate desire. But we are only able to make a difference through and in direct relationship with others. Tom realized he was no longer making an intentional difference—he had stayed in his role too long; his job no longer fit him. That is when he decided he would have to end his relationship with a company he had resurrected with his innovative ideas and products. That was the insight Tom got about himself and how he works best—the difference he was made to make, he realized, was to resurrect dying organizations. Leading a successful maturing one, as this one had become, bored him, even frustrated him. Tom resigned—for his good and that of the company.

Stephen Covey in his book *The 7 Habits of Highly Effective People* says one of the habits of successful people is gaining insight. In his words, it is "seek[ing] first to understand . . . then to be understood."[16] Highly effective people seek insight. To gain insight into another requires being attentive to that person—studying them. You have to intentionally focus on the person.

Judith Martens, Innovation and Research Officer at Sugar Habits, explains Covey's statement this way in her blog:

> Covey explicitly puts a focus on listening *by heart*, which goes further than techniques can take you.
>
> Another person—your lover, employee or someone you just met—will notice that you are sincerely interested if he or she experiences that you are listening honestly.
>
> Only by listening sincerely will you notice the true feelings and ideas of your friend or colleague.[17]

We notice new and deeper things about a person the more we study them. Take the case of Max Trotz, a young manager of a Walgreens store who turned his attention toward studying an underperforming employee working the store floor. Max noticed the employee seemed to be trying, but she was never where she should be at the time she should be there. He wondered if being a little overweight or a little older than some of the other employees working on the store floor was the reason why she seemed to always be lagging behind and never quite catching up.

As he continued to study her, he observed that she seemed friendly toward the people who came in, always happy to chat with everyone. But, he concluded, she could not be allowed to continue at her low level of performance—she was too slow helping customers find what they needed and always a little behind stocking the shelves. She simply was not good enough at her job to succeed in the busy all-purpose pharmacy and household goods outlet. Max, even as a new manager at the time, had the uncanny insight that distinguishes highly effective people from others. Max continued to observe her for a few weeks, and then one day, an idea occurred to him—he put her behind a cash register.

Seven thousand Walgreens executives gave a collective gasp during my speech at their annual conference when I told them that Max had done this. In their experience, no seasoned manager would have encouraged an unqualified, failing employee to interact with customers. But an insightful manager would and did. Almost immediately after Max made his move, everyone could see the difference. Behind the register, his employee didn't have to run around, and there, her social skills were a positive asset. She was a natural at asking after customers' needs and making smart suggestions. In just a few months, she became one of the district's top suggestive sellers.

Simply by studying her in the context of her abilities and then repositioning her, Max helped her progress from a below-average employee to an exceptional one. Max used his insight and by doing so optimized a Relationship-Impacting Opportunity. In the same way, Tom and his people became more successful as an organization as they began to study each other in terms of how to increase performance.

How insightful are you? Is there a work or personal relationship that you need to look at in a deeper way? One that needs to end for the good of all involved? I have provided three questions below to help you process:

1. How well does your difference align with the person(s) with whom you are in relationship?

2. Have you studied the person to get to really know them?

3. Would having insight about yours and their six dimensions help you make a more informed choice whether to enhance or end your relationship?

Consider again the quotes at the beginning of the chapter. Both husband and wife identified and understood what caused the positive change in the wife's ability and willingness to express her thoughts and feelings. They had insight into the situation.

How can you deepen your relationships with similar insight? And when you gain insight into yourself and the people you study, how will that affect your mission?

Freddie is more than a brother; he is one of my partners in life. I do not make a major decision without his input. He never made it to college, but he has an advanced degree in practical advice. He is my baby brother, but I look up to him. Out of the ten siblings, he is the glue that holds the family together.

—OLDER BROTHER

I discovered an important thing a while ago about my older brother: my opinion counts to him. When he was getting married, he asked for my opinion and took my advice about how much to budget for the wedding. When he felt it was time to change careers, he asked for input on whether to go back to school or not. He agreed with me and has a master's degree and a professional career today as a result. He is my best friend. I would do anything for him.

—YOUNGER BROTHER

CHAPTER NINE

ESSENTIAL YOU: ENSURING OPINIONS MATTER IN RELATIONSHIPS

Shared opinion is an indispensable ingredient; in fact, it is the lifeblood of any relationship. When opinions stop flowing freely and constructively, the relationship is in danger. The greatest danger lies not just in the unwillingness to share opinions with the other person in the relationship but in a willingness to share that opinion with others outside of the relationship. This was the case, you may recall, in Tom's organization—employees stopped sharing their opinion with Tom and his leadership team but instead made it a point to share their opinion with the Board.

Opinions matter more or less based upon whose they are. Those that matter most to us come from people with whom we have a good relationship. Those that count less come from those with whom we have less of a relationship. Strangers do not have permission to tell us what we should or should not do. Likewise, we heed or regard less the opinions of people who are not strangers but with whom we have a strained or distant relationship.

Opinions, in this way, are an indication of the health and depth of a relationship. The degree to which there is relationship is the degree to which permission is given for opinions to be expressed and received. Opinions require permission. Without permission, opinions are an annoyance, intrusion, or presumption. We have to give others permission before we accept an opinion. On the other hand, once we grant permission, we confirm the other person's value to us.

In the same way, we know when they share their opinions with us, they care for us. In relationships—when it comes to opinions—sharing is caring. This is what we see demonstrated by the two brothers in the quote at the beginning of the chapter—they value each other.

Along these lines, we will focus now upon an Intentional Relationship as the *uplifting use of opinion* to create and maintain a mutual and selfless connection. In this chapter, you will learn how to use opinion in a way to assess and increase the value you and others bring to your relationships.

BEHAVIOR #5: SHARE

RIO: CREATE AN OPINION-SAFE RELATIONSHIP.

No intentional relationship exists without the free-flowing soliciting and giving of opinions. Spouses who do not seek to get or give an opinion have long ago checked out of the marriage. Siblings who never think to offer input to or solicit input from their brother or sister are related mostly by blood, not by practice. Managers and employees who would rather not get or give feedback are disengaged employees. On the other hand, employees, spouses, siblings, and, for that matter, anyone who would offer their good-intentioned opinion are likely engaged at work and in their relationships. This is because they are psychologically and emotionally committed to their roles within that relationship. They care about the success of the organization and they care about the other person. The Gallup Organization refers to employees who feel free to share their opinions as "internal stock" value. Gallup reports that an employee's freedom to express opinions "measures the sense of value that employees feel in their work and toward their organization."[18] Internal stock value is Gallup's way of saying employee opinion is of great value to an organization.

Opinions matter. They matter to the person who has an opinion to share, and they matter to the person who has benefited from, or would or could benefit from, a well-placed, timely opinion that averts disaster. In this way, opinions may reveal how much people care about each other.

How about you? Do you care enough about the people at work or at home to share your opinions? Do you have people who care enough about you to share their opinions? Has permission been granted in your relationships for opinions to be shared? Is this an instance where you have the qualifications, experience, expertise, or simply enough information to have a valid opinion?

These are the type of questions that had to be answered as we helped Tom and his people understand how to use opinion in an uplifting and intentional way.

Relationships in Tom's organization were not ones where people volunteered their opinions. This was a problem, one that we discovered increased the danger for emergency personnel in the field. For example, whenever a weather crisis occurred, the call came into the inbound-call operators, informing them of the emergency services needed. They then passed along those needs to the outbound-call operator who dispatched personnel and equipment. Both groups did their jobs—to an extent; information was passed along efficiently and accurately.

During the short-lived focus groups we conducted, inbound operators admitted to holding back opinions that may have helped the other team know the severity or nuance of the emergency situation. We asked them for an example of how they held back their opinion. They told us it may have been as simple as the tone or the words that the caller used that alerted the experienced inbound operator that something more was afoot, that there was additional risk involved.

Depending on whether or not the outbound operator was "friendly" or not, the decision was made to share or hold back the intuitive opinion. Most times, too many times, that decision to hold back an opinion borne out of experience impacted crucial decisions that may have made the difference between life and death for a person. When we asked why they made such a choice, knowing how critical the impact could be, the consistent response was, "I did not feel my opinion mattered." The fact is, given the unhealthy relationships that existed in Tom's organization according to who was in the conversation, opinions probably did not matter.

Our opinions might or might not matter to the other person, writes Kevin A. Thompson on his blog, *Opinions Rarely Matter*:

When it comes to your life, your decisions, and your actions, my opinions do not really matter.

They might matter if you care. If you desire to know my thoughts or ideas and you ask to hear them, then they might matter.

But if we don't have much of a relationship or even if we do and you don't care about my thoughts on this area of your life, then my opinions don't matter.[19]

So how do you get better at using opinion in an uplifting way? Thompson provides a guide on how to go about deciding if and when to share opinions. He writes:

Before sharing your opinion with anyone, consider these questions:

1. Do I have all the information necessary to have an opinion?
2. Do I have the right motives for sharing my opinion?
3. If I share this opinion, am I sharing it with the right person?
4. Do I have the proper relationship to have a right to share my opinion?
5. If the situation was reversed, would I be happy if this opinion was shared with me?

What question would you add in order to determine the right time to share your opinions?[20]

To have an opinion is a personal responsibility. You alone must decide to share or not to share. For every opinion you have, you are faced with the question: how do I use my opinion in a way that is beneficial to the other person and not harmful to me?

To share an opinion requires self-examination—of your feelings, motives, and resulting behavior. Tom and his people got there; they got to the point where they did the self-examining process of discovering why important, mission-related opinions were not being shared. People did not know if, when, or how to share important opinions. What they discovered is what is true in all relationships: each person contributes to an environment where it is either safe or not safe for opinions to be shared.

In your relationships, is it safe enough to share your opinion? How safe have you made it for others to share their opinion with you? To be successful in building an intentional relationship, we must learn how to use opinion in an uplifting way. Boston University has a six-step guideline for providing constructive feedback that we have tailored slightly to help people be intentional in how they share opinions:

1. If you can't think of a constructive purpose for expressing your opinion, don't. Focus on encouragement rather than judgment.

2. Describing behavior is a way of reporting what has occurred, while judging behavior is an evaluation of what has occurred in terms of "right or wrong" or "good or bad." By avoiding evaluative language, you reduce the need for the individual to respond defensively. For example: "You demonstrate a high degree of confidence when you answer customer questions about registration procedures" rather than "Your communication skills are good."

3. Focus on observation rather than inference. Observations refer to what you can see or hear about an

individual's behavior, while inferences refer to the assumptions and interpretations you make from what you see or hear. Focus on what the person did and your reaction. For example: "When you gave that student the financial aid form, you tossed it across the counter" rather than describing what you assume to be the person's motivation: "I suppose you give all forms out that way!"

4. Focus on behavior rather than the person. Refer to what an individual does rather than on what you imagine she or he is. To focus on behavior, use adverbs, which describe action, rather than adjectives, which describe qualities. For example: "You talked extensively during the staff meeting, which prevented me from getting to some of the main points" rather than "You talk too much."

5. Provide a balance of positive and negative feedback. If you consistently give only positive or negative feedback, people will distrust the feedback and it will become useless.

6. Be aware of feedback overload. Select two or three important points you want to make and offer feedback about those points. If you overload an individual with feedback, she or he may become confused about what needs to be improved or changed. For example: "The number of applicants and the time it takes you to enter them are both within the expected ranges. However, the number of keying errors you are currently making is higher than expected."[21]

Learning how to share your opinion constructively benefits both parties in a relationship. Done right, sharing an opinion can open up a nourishing and rewarding exchange for both persons. It certainly did for Tom and his leadership team. Once they began building intentional relationships, intentional conversations increased. As a result, employees began offering opinions that were long held but never communicated. Most of them were practical ideas about how to improve a process or response in emergency situations. One such opinion held by an outbound operator concerned how emergency staff was treated.

"In my opinion," she said, "there is an easy way to increase response time from the emergency responders in the field."

When pressed to say how, she went on to explain how over the years she had heard many of the emergency personnel express concern for their own families left without electricity during stormy weather. In her opinion, the company should provide those who were likely to be called out during an emergency situation with portable generators. This, she said, would do two things: provide some peace of mind to the employee and demonstrate that the organization cared enough to do such a thing.

When this operator expressed her insightful opinion, it increased the understanding of the leadership team concerning their staff. And the simple solution increased the trust and proficiency of the employees.

Opinions are an opportunity to share information. However, information is not the only thing, or even the most important thing, that is shared when someone expresses an opinion. Risk and trust are also shared. One risk for the person offering an opinion is that his opinion may be rejected. A risk for the receiver of the opinion is in accepting the opinion and using it to make a decision. An expressed opinion is about trust: does one person trust the other to take one of these risks? Relationships thrive or die because of trust.

Sharing an opinion is one way to assess the amount of trust that exists in relationship. Do you trust the person you are in relationship with enough to share what you really think? Do they trust you enough to allow you the freedom to spontaneously share your opinion without shutting you out in response?

Opinions matter in relationship. They matter because they can help you determine whether you have a healthy, dying, or nonexistent relationship.

To help you start using opinion to evaluate your relationship, answer these two questions:

1. Is your relationship one where your opinion is allowed or valued?

2. Do you allow and value the opinion of the other person in your relationship?

If you answered yes for either one of these questions, there is hope, and you can start to work on your relationship by intentionally reinforcing your openness in offering and receiving opinions and by re-reading and applying SECRET from the intentional conversation chapter. If the answer is no for both questions, your relationship is dying or already nonexistent.

In summary, opinions are:

- A measurement of the health of a relationship
- An opportunity to share information, risk, and trust
- An opening for nourishing and rewarding conversations
- An indispensable ingredient, the lifeblood of a relationship
- An uplifting way to add value and depth to a relationship

Take this time to reflect on what you have learned in this chapter about how to use opinion to evaluate your relationship. As you determine where you are, I offer you two challenges: Create the safety and bond necessary to become someone whose opinions count by telling someone today that their opinion matters to you. And then invite those to whom you have granted permission to share more of their opinions with you.

When Tom is in the room, people notice his presence. When Melissa is absent from the discussion, we miss her analytical input and questions. Some people just have presence. I am not one of those persons. At parties, I just fade into the wallpaper—most people would not even know I attended.

—MARK

It is true Melissa and I have our unique presence. But Mark—his presence is quiet and powerful. He hardly ever talks, but on the rare occasion that he does, his is the voice of wisdom. Clients and employees alike refer to him as Gandalf, the wise and noble wizard from the Lord of the Rings.

—TOM

CHAPTER TEN

INFLUENTIAL YOU: MAKING YOUR PRESENCE FELT IN RELATIONSHIPS

"What is your most important task as a manager?" I asked during a meeting with the managers in Tom's organization. The answers the group came up with were more or less just what I expected. Some said their first job was to ensure that the organization's interest was protected and promoted. Others replied that they wanted most to help employees get their work done in efficient and productive ways. Still others responded that their highest responsibility was to select quality employees. Then, as the responses quieted down, one lady in the back of the room spoke up, quietly but assertively.

"To use our influence to improve relationships with our employees, each other, and our customers."

There was a hushed silence. No one moved. It seemed that everyone was holding their breath. Then that breath came out in a collective sigh: "Wow."

That was it exactly! The manager's most important task and tool is influence—managers influence people. The same is true for everyone in a relationship; we influence others.

BEHAVIOR #6: INFLUENCE

RIO: INSTIGATE GROWTH EVENTS.

Everyone has physical presence. Wherever we are, we occupy space. Psychological and social presence, however, such as Mark described in the quotes at the beginning of the chapter, is something that each person needs to learn how to recognize and develop. In this chapter, the focus is upon intentional relationship as the uplifting *use of influence* to create and maintain a mutual and selfless connection with another person. In this chapter, we will discuss how to exert influence in a way that improves your relationships at home and at work.

In an intentional relationship, people influence each other in an uplifting way to bring about significant personal change for themselves and for others. For most people, however, using influence is a very difficult thing to do. Kerry Patterson, Joseph Grenny, David Maxfield, Ron McMillan, and Al Switzler in their book *Influencer: The Power to Change Anything* explain why exerting influence is a hard thing for most people.

Fortunately you've learned to follow the words of a well-known prayer: Every day you ask for the serenity to accept the things you cannot change, the courage to change the things you can't, and the wisdom to know the difference. Somehow that gets you through. And that's the problem. It's everyone's problem. We've come to believe that when we face enormous challenges that can be solved only by influencing intractable behaviors, we might attempt a couple of change strategies. When they fail miserably, we surrender. It's time to move on. We tell ourselves that we're not influencers, and that it's time to turn our attention to things that are in our control. We seek serenity.[22]

The authors are referring to the serenity prayer attributed to Reinhold Niebuhr. Their position is that people too readily seek serenity when they should instead be using the power of influence to bring about solutions. Everybody has influence: you do, I do, we all do. The problem is, according to these authors, we fail to recognize our power to influence others because of how we think.

We typically don't think of ourselves as influencers because we fail to see that the common thread running through most of the triumphs and tragedies of our lives is our ability to exert influence. If we did, we'd invest enormous energy in looking for new and better ways to enhance our influence repertoire.[23]

Do you have influence in your relationship? In your relationships, are you aware of how influence is at work? How are you exerting influence? How are others influencing you?

These are very important questions, for they are about presence—your presence in a relationship. Our presence matters to those with whom we are in relationship. They care that we are around. More than that, according to how healthy the relationship is, they want us in their life and career—they want our participation, our influence.

Think about that for a minute: what difference does your presence make at home or at work? Do people in your life and at your workplace care and want you around? Who are they? Why do they care? These were difficult questions for the managers in Tom's organization to answer. They were difficult in the sense that the answers were painfully revealing of how managers had misused their influence. They had used their influence for so long to deride and demean each other that it was clear that employees generally did not value or revere the management team as a whole.

As a result, their ability to influence positive change—good behavior and increased performance—was, at first, limited. But all of that changed once they began building intentional relationships. Instead of being an unwanted presence, employees began to recognize and accept encouragement and input from their own managers and those from other teams. Presence and influence go together—you have to be a recognized and accepted presence in order to exert influence in an uplifting way.

Tom realized this, and he purposefully worked on changing how his presence was felt by his leadership and management teams. In his remaining months at the company, he intentionally stopped misusing his influence. In the past, it was his practice to circumvent his executives whenever there was a delay in emergency response time by going directly to the manager of the group. This was traumatic to the manager and the team because Tom would yell and threaten them with the loss of their jobs. Tom came to own his misbehavior and did two things to change it:

HE CHANGED THE WAY HE MADE HIS PRESENCE FELT AND HE USED HIS INFLUENCE INTENTIONALLY TO DO GOOD.

Your presence is being felt in some way right now in your relationships. It may be as disruptive as Tom's or as unassuming as Mark's in the quotes from the beginning of the chapter. In any case, you need to know how your presence is being felt in order to use influence in an uplifting way.

To begin with, know that the way you present yourself is a learned behavior—you make your presence felt based upon what you've learned in the past. Who has been or is a physically present person who has had tremendous influence upon your life? What was their influence like? What words describe their influence upon you?

Some time ago, I asked these questions during a discussion with Dr. Rudy Lewis, my former boss and mentor. We were driving back from an appointment with a client in Ada, Oklahoma, and had some time before I had to catch a flight. Upon hearing my questions, Rudy suggested we take a detour to the small town of Stratford, where he grew up. Once there, he pointed at a rather rundown building.

"That," he said, "was where I had my first real job." As we looked out at the building, Rudy, an experienced higher-education upper management professional who serves as a consultant to Fortune 500 companies proceeded to answer my questions by sharing an example of how someone's influence impacted his life:

"H. B. Mount," Rudy explained, saying the name of the owner of the ramshackle building. "That building used to house the most prestigious men's clothing store in this small town of Stratford. People would come to shop in that store from all over Oklahoma. After returning home from military service, I was still very green and without any work experience, per se. When I noticed a 'Help wanted' sign in the store window, I went to Mr. Mount and asked him for the job."

Rudy paused at that point, obviously remembering a moment that was of great importance to him.

"To my surprise, he put me to work the very next day," he said, picking up the thread of his tale. "I was surprised because at the time Mr. Mount hired me, it must have been obvious to him that I did not know the first thing about dressing. At the time, I did not own a suit or a decent pair of dress shoes. However, in spite of my rough edges and inexperience, he picked me. Mr. Mount believed in me. He took time to teach me the business and how to dress. He polished me up. Most importantly, Mr. Mount invested his time and resources in an unselfish way to help me. Over time, he greatly influenced how I dressed and presented myself.

"A few years later, after I had graduated from college and was still working for him part time, Mr. Mount learned of my political aspirations. This is why I thought of him when you started talking about influence. I count him as one of the most influential people in my life. He shaped who I am today. Mr. Mount volunteered his time, money, and network to help me campaign. It was because of him that I was elected to the school board, and because of that entrée, I went on to make a career in education. Mr. Mount helped me realize my dream." As Rudy explained all this to me, his voice filled with respect. "Because of people like him, I am honored to play a very small part, if any, in helping others realize theirs."

I tell this story because it illustrates the ongoing impact of influence. Mr. Mount influenced Rudy, and Rudy influenced me. Influence is like that: it is a gift that keeps on giving. But in order to give the gift of influence, you need to monitor and manage *your presence.*

So here are three questions to ask yourself to help you understand your influence:

1. How do you make your presence felt in your relationships?
2. In your relationships, what are the ways you influence?
3. How can you modify your presence in order to use your influence to uplift more?

If any of these questions are hard to answer, it probably means you need more help understanding how to use influence.

Here is a quick mental checklist to use when faced with an opportunity to influence others:

1. In the present situation, what value do I bring?
2. If I choose to withhold my influence in the present instance, is any injury done to me, to others, or to the organization?

3. In the present instance, are others counting on me to influence their decision?

In your relationships, ask yourself often: what is my influencing territory? Then claim your territory. Get it clearly in your mind what activity and in what situations you tend to be at your influential best. You may use these three strengths-identifying questions to help you pinpoint where you influence best:

1. Is this a situation where others ask me to take charge?

2. When I have exerted my influence, in this type of instance, have I gotten my best results?

3. Are there instances or activities where I would gladly exert influence more often?

It is also important to ask: "What do I see in the mirror?" If you examine your history closely, you are likely to discover a pattern of how you have influenced others. For some of you, the pattern involves challenging or crisis situations at work, as was the case for Tom. For others, it may involve situations where you come to the rescue or intervene on behalf of others. Still for others, it may be encouraging and praising your children. Whatever your pattern of influence, you need to know it in order to use influence to the fullest in your relationships.

One last question to ask is: "Am I using my influence enough?" Your influence can help others discover and unleash their potential, as Mr. Mount did for Rudy and as Rudy did for me. Be driven to help others learn to step up and lead at the appropriate time. Urge others to act.

Take inventory with these questions so you can know for sure if you are using your influence enough:

1. In your relationship(s) within the last six months, have you helped someone discover new opportunities for growth or increased success?

2. At work, is there a relationship where you have been reluctant or absentminded in your use of influence?

3. If you were given only one opportunity to influence, who would you influence to do what? Why?

Influence is a gift you give to yourself and others. You do it by making your presence felt in an uplifting way.

If, in your relationship, you have done all you can to add value and your influence is still minimal or ignored, you may want to consider if it's time for you to move on. At work, it may mean that, like Tom, you have outgrown the role or outlived your welcome. In your personal life, it may mean the relationship has run its course or you have failed to or refused to take the risks of building an intentional relationship. Do you invest the time and effort to make the present relationship better or do you end it?

If you have not built an intentional relationship, I recommend investing the time doing so; I know from personal experience that there is great reward in return. And part of that is changing your influence to uplift the others in your relationships.

So stop now and write out your patterns of influence. What are they? Who have you impacted? What more could you have done?

Now consider where your pattern of influence can grow. What do you want to accomplish? Who do you want to reach? What more can you do?

Finally, ask yourself how you can effect that change. What can you do now to uplift another by the power of your influence today? This week? This month?

I look back on my last face-to-face interaction with my mom, and I miss her. I had stopped by to visit her on my way to speak at a conference in Orlando, Florida. I walked up to her door, dressed in my suit and tie, and when she opened the door, she gave me that same warm smile that I had long ago come to love, the same smile I got from her anytime she was going to surprise me for my birthday or with that special toy I wanted for Christmas. This smile, too, was to be a special gift to me.

"You knock 'em dead, don't you?" she said, looking me over in my business attire. "I can see you take control. That's what we saw in you as a baby," my mother said to me. "Your dad and I knew you were going to be special, more special than all the rest."

In that moment, I knew that I was special only because my adopted parents had chosen to give me their very special kind of love, the kind of love that comes only from sincere and committed parents.

My mother died one week later. My father had died fourteen years prior, but they left me with a unique gift: the gift of self-worth. She looked at me, her son, that day, and she passed the baton. It was as if she was signing off. Her mission—"rescue the throw-away kid"—had been accomplished.

—SON

CHAPTER ELEVEN

COMPASSIONATE YOU: FORGING SELFLESS CONNECTION IN RELATIONSHIPS

Serving others, whether out of a heart of love or self-preservation, still makes perfectly good sense today—it is mutually beneficial. The Board made Tom and his employees aware of that fact, but changing the way the staff treated each other was driven by a deeper *emotional* need—the need to care and to be cared for in return. As things changed, people in different teams and cliques grew to care for one another; they actually built intentional relationships.

In an earlier chapter, I said sharing is caring—serving is also caring. It's easy to care about someone you serve. It's also easy to serve someone when you care about him or her.

BEHAVIOR #7: SERVE

RIO: INITIATE SELFLESSNESS BY DOING GOOD.

A relationship is about giving and receiving. It is about being served and serving others. The adopted son, in the quote at the start of the chapter, expressed how receiving service from his parents blessed him, but he also blessed them. Theirs was an intentional relationship of giving and receiving service.

This chapter is about how to create and maintain *a mutual and selfless connection* with another person. In this chapter, you will learn strategies for bringing out the best in the person(s) with whom you are in relationship.

RIOs are pivotal moments when we make the choice to serve self or to serve others. I've offered many business-related experiences that have highlighted how to impact your relationship for the better, but now I'd like to share an example of pure service—albeit at work—when Mic Adams built a selfless connection by serving another in a very powerful, very intentional RIO.

> "I had just started my career as a physical therapist when I came in contact with a young boy who had been in a horrible car accident," Mic Adams—a burly, warm-hearted physical therapist—stated as he shared his story with me. "He'd had a head injury that rendered him comatose with serious damage that his doctors were saying was permanent. I volunteered to work with him, to help move his legs to keep his muscles from atrophying and to keep his legs supple.
>
> "The boy couldn't wake up from that coma, and over a period of three years, doctors tried different procedures

to help him. One procedure in particular seemed to hold great promise, but after two failed attempts, the doctors declared him beyond recovery. Permanently comatose."

But Mic refused to see improvement as impossible. He kept looking for the next step that would take that boy, his patient, just one step more toward possible.

"As I continued to work with the patient," Mic recalled, "I found myself reading about these kinds of brain injuries. Looking at the research, I learned what new procedures were being tested. Finally, I suggested to his mother that we find a surgeon that would put a shunt in the boy's brain. She agreed, and we began our search. We found a doctor who had developed a new procedure that had proven effective on other patients. He agreed to take this boy on, and he implanted the shunt in his poor, injured head. Two weeks later, after being in a coma for three years, the boy awakened.

"It was truly amazing," Mic concluded. "To see that boy come back to life, as it were, was absolutely fascinating. I am extremely fortunate to have been a part of that miracle for the boy and his family."

Mic did not give up. He could not shake the idea that something, even something seemingly impossible, could happen for the boy and his parents. Such is the power of a selfless connection.

Sounds utopic, right? It does, but miraculous stories like Mic's happen often when people become intentional in their relationships. The miraculous always happens when we serve others. Sometimes the miracle is as simple as someone getting help with what they could not do for themselves. Every time, the miracle is that we break free from the restraints of only serving self. That is the motivation for building an intentional relationship: to serve others.

But an intentional relationship is also reciprocal—we serve and we are served. This is the singularly most important characteristic of an intentional relationship—mutual service to one another.

Think about your relationships: who serves whom? As a manager, who serves—you or your employee? As a spouse, who serves? As a parent, son, or daughter, who serves? You get the picture—in a relationship each person *ought to be* serving the other person. In an intentional relationship, everyone does. Simple concept. Yet difficult and unlikely to be the case in most relationships.

Sometimes, as was the case for Tom and his company, we need to start by providing an incentive for service. We proposed to the Board that Tom and his team were rewarded with a bonus based on the improvement to company culture and interaction. With that motivation spurring change, soon the incentive was unnecessary because the culture had adapted enough that service and the benefits of it were enough to motivate the entire staff to intentionally develop mutual and selfless connections.

Benjamin Fairless, in the passage below, offers some controversial and provocative advice on how to get more people serving each other:

> As far as I know, there are only two basic motivations that cause you and me and other people to serve our neighbors voluntarily and regularly. One, of course, is the moral code found in the teachings of our Judeo-Christian religion. . . .The other motivation that causes us to

serve our fellow men is the desire to get something in return from them.

It is sometimes said that when service is motivated by charity and love, it is good; but that when the motivation is materialistic, it is bad. Well, I'm going to challenge the second part of that concept. I'm going to explore the possibility that the desire to earn a profit may cause us to serve more people—more effectively—than does our desire to be charitable. . . .

Stop and think with me for a moment as to what would happen to you—or to me or anyone else—if no one helped us in any way.

I assure you that if no one helped me, my standard of living would soon plummet to near zero. Literally, if other people refused to share their talents and skills with me, I would soon perish. I'm just not capable of being my own doctor, making my own clothing, and growing my own food. Even though I'm an engineer, I still can't generate my own electricity, build my own house, and do the ten-thousand-and-one other things that make life both possible and pleasant.

If for no other reason, self-interest alone would cause me to offer my poor talents in the service of other people in order to persuade them to help me.[24]

While I agree with Fairless that we would suffer, at large, without self-interested service, I think that we can only gain so much from universal and impersonal service such as he describes. I gain much more when I interact with the people who serve me and whom I serve. In fact, I can boldly claim that when I intentionally serve, I learn to serve more out of charity, caring for the other person, than I do for personal gain or satisfaction.

So how can you serve effectively in your relationships? Here are four actions and reasons we shared with Tom and his employees that will help you know how you serve others:

1. Identify "why" a relationship is important to you
   - To serve another person requires a compelling reason

2. Understand "who" you become because of the relationship
   - To serve another person requires an accepted identity

3. Discover "how" your personality is activated in the relationship
   - To serve another person requires bringing a unique contribution

4. Define "what" an intentional relationship does for you
   - To serve another person requires clarifying the outcomes

WHY?

To serve another person requires a compelling reason—one that ignites your willingness to serve. Think about one of your relationships; what is the reason you serve that person? Maslow's hierarchy of needs[25] is a useful tool in this instance. Start with what he calls "basic needs." Are you serving because doing so provides physical sustenance and safety, such as food, water,

gainful occupation, etc.? If you respond in terms of your relationships at work, with your boss and coworkers, the answer is "Yes,
of course." But what about personal relationships? Do they also
provide needs? Absolutely; however, those needs are likely to be
higher up on Maslow's scale, such as a need to love and be loved, a
need to belong, and a need for self-esteem and self-actualization.

Too often in relationships at work and at home, we are less
aware of what is driving us to be in a relationship. Understanding
which compelling need we are satisfying through a relationship
will help us clarify our motive.

"Ouch!" you may say. "I only tolerate my manager because
they pay me." Or "I realize now I am only in this relationship
because of the 'benefits' I receive." At this time, perhaps your
manager is only fulfilling your basic need to be able to buy food
and afford rent. But if you want to deepen that relationship, it
could also fulfill your need for self-esteem or respect.

Asking "why" will help you clarify and, hopefully, purify your
motives. For to have an intentional relationship is to create and
maintain a mutual and selfless connection with another person.

Tom and his people were surprised to discover that their jobs
actually did much more than provide for their physical and safety
needs. They actually wanted to be loved and cared for by their
managers and coworkers. They wanted to belong to a healthy
team. Fortunately for them, as they learned to build healthier
relationships, safety, self-esteem, love, respect, and self-actualization increased for all of them.

Think about that a bit; let that sink in. Relationships are *that*
important to you, to who you are, and to who you are becoming. Every need, basic or higher on Maslow's scale, is likely to be
met directly through your relationships with other people. You

do not, nor can you, satisfy your own needs as a human in isolation; you need other people. Serving others helps you satisfy your human needs.

Take stock of your relationships; why do you need them? Simply put, you need each and every one to help you become the person you are meant to be. We need to serve so that we can grow into who we can be through our relationships.

Which leads to the second lesson we taught Tom and his group: understand "who" you are in the relationship.

WHO?

To serve another person requires an accepted identity. Each person in a relationship has a "relationship identity." On one level, this identity is established, such as parent, offspring, sibling, manager, employee, etc. On a deeper, less obvious level, there is an identity I accept as a way of serving the other person. You could be the people-pleaser, the tell-it-like-it-is person, or the there-in-a-pinch friend. For example, I know a person who describes herself as the "good child."

"I am the good child because my parents know they can ask me to do the most ridiculous or inconvenient tasks at all hours of night or day and I will do it. My other siblings tell them no. I hate being used like that—but I feel guilty feeling this way about my parents."

This person is having a relationship identity crisis. This could be you, too, if you have not taken the time to understand who you are in your relationships. You may have accepted an identity that does you harm, as in the case of the person I just mentioned.

An intentional relationship requires that you know who you are in serving other people. Remember, it is an uplifting, mutual, and selfless connection with another person. You may need an extreme makeover if the relationship is not mutually uplifting. Chapter Six, on understanding personalities, can help you begin sorting out the role you want to claim.

Tom came to this place of filling an inauthentic role in his life and career when he realized that his personality was no longer aligned with the tasks he was being asked to do. Understanding who you are in a relationship will help you decide whether to continue to serve or end a relationship. And it also teaches you how your personality is activated in your relationship.

HOW?

To serve another person requires bringing your unique contribution. Regardless of the relationship you are in, you are there because of who you are. Understanding how you make a difference is important in order to determine how you serve.

> The Gallup Organization has a practice of requiring that each employee recruit and commission a personal board of directors. The process involves identifying and recruiting people who have a vested interest in your career to be on your board. On one such occasion, an employee had brought together his board and began the meeting by asking each person one question. The one question was: "Why did I choose you to be on this board?"
>
> People were caught off guard; they expected the employee to tell them why he had chosen them for his board.

He insisted upon an answer. They did the best they could to answer. Once everyone had attempted to respond, the employee told each person not why they were there but how they were already contributing and, he hoped, would continue to contribute to his career. One such board member was his best friend, Ken Lee. The conversation went like this:

Employee: Ken, what do you do for me?

Ken: Well, I am your friend.

Employee: Yes, you are my best friend. But what do you do for me?

Ken: I am not sure of your question, but I guess I help you where I can.

Employee: Yes, you do. But more specifically, here is how you help me and why you are on my board of directors. Remember when I mentioned to you last year that we needed to replace our family car? I told you how the kids were ashamed of the old, beat-up "grocery picker," they called it, because it has a practice of breaking down right in front of their school. So I really needed to buy a more dependable car.

Ken: Yeah, now I remember. I remember that car . . . you picked me up from the airport in it. I remember thinking that I should have caught a cab. (Laughing.)

Employee: That was my favorite car, mostly because it only cost me two hundred and fifty dollars. But here is why you are here. Once I told you that I was looking for a car, you said, "Okay, I will get back to you next week." The next week I received a UPS box filled with documents. One document was a consumer report providing information about the safest, most fuel efficient, cost-effective, and highest-retained-resale-value family van. Ken Lee, that is how you contribute; you are unique on this board. Your role is to bring that same meticulous, research-oriented, fact-finding propensity to the goals and aspirations I share with you concerning my career.

Ken: I can do that. That's what I do.

Find how you serve others in your relationships, making your unique contribution. Only you can bring what you have inside you to your relationships. And that is how others will count upon you to serve them. To dig deeper into what your unique contribution is, refer to Chapter Eight, the section that defines the six dimensions of your intentional difference. For now, let's continue onto the last action and reason for how you serve: defining "what" an intentional relationship does for you.

WHAT?

To serve another person requires clarifying the outcomes. What do you expect from serving others? Serving others leaves an indelible imprint. We remember people who serve us well. Likewise, when we serve others, they are likely to remember us. Serving involves what we get and what we give.

As I was writing this book, I reached out to Tom's old organization. I spoke briefly with Sam, a former colleague of Tom. Sam told me the organization is growing by "leaps and bounds." He commented that many of the ideas and strategies Tom implemented are still a part of their process and practice. Most notably, the ideas and strategies of building intentional relationships is still prominent there. Tom is still remembered there, mostly for how much he had personally changed in the last year.

I also reached out to Tom. He instantly recalled the change he experienced at his old organization. During our phone call, he spilled out a description of how hard, mean, and intimidating he was. But it was not with sadness; it was with gratitude. Tom has completely changed his approach to relationships. In fact, his current full-time job is helping other CEOs and executives who are, in his words, "like I used to be: hard-nosed, self-centered, hard-driving machines, oblivious to what it means to be in an intentional relationship with another human being."

Serving others is about what you get—not in a selfish, ego-centric way but in a karmic, reciprocal way. What you get is a new and improved you. Serving others really serves you. Some level of denying of self is required in order to use your personality, conversation, insight, opinion, and influence to serve others in an uplifting way. The more you serve, the more refined you become. Through serving others, you get a better you. Tom certainly did.

In an intentional relationship, serving others is not only about how much you get but also about how much of yourself you give. And that brings us to the second part of serving—what you give. What you give is time. No relationship exists without time spent together. Relationships demand that we spend time with the other person(s). In fact, the quality of your relationship is directly impacted by time spent. The impact, however, comes not from *how much time is spent* but rather from *what the time is spent doing.*

Before our work began, Tom's people had grown to want less and less time in his presence. Time spent with Tom, they said, was time spent being criticized and reprimanded. They dreaded and hated those meetings. Ironically, Tom was planning on scheduling even more time with them. He was oblivious to how deeply managers despised his mandated weekly one-on-one, two-hour meetings. He told us he felt his most effective and meaningful times were his meetings with staff. Over the months as we worked with Tom, we helped him to learn that spending time with others should focus not on *what you want* but more upon finding out *what they need*. By the end, as you have observed, Tom learned how to serve; managers and employees were benefiting from uplifting time spent with him.

So how are you using time in your relationship? What is the time spent doing? Is time spent in an uplifting way? Do you spend time when and how others need it from you? Do you plan how you will spend time with them? Is the time spent serving them or serving you? How are you giving time?

An intentional relationship is about giving yourself away to serve others. Once you do that, serving opens up your capacity to become more of what you can be. It's an indisputable law of God and man that when you give, "you will receive. Your gift will return to you in full, pressed down, shaken together to make room for more, running over, and poured into your lap. The amount you give will determine the amount you get back."[26]

Standing outside, looking through the bars, I can see Charlie sitting on the slab of concrete that represented his bed—Her Majesty's Prison provided few comforts for inmates. He rose when I approached his cell. I am moved by the peace I see on his face. And I am instantly reminded that our three years of friendship is about to come to an end tomorrow at 7 a.m., eastern time.

What a journey we had together! He and I sometimes talking quietly about life, death, and the hereafter. At other times, we got caught up in heated debate over which team would make it to the playoffs. And sometimes, I just listened as he related what he had read over the past week that struck a chord with him. I watched Charlie change from an angry, violent, hateful twenty-two-year-old boy into a peaceful, thoughtful, and penitent twenty-five-year-old condemned convict.

—COUNSELOR

Charlie, my cell neighbor and good friend, stopped by my cell this morning. He was at peace on his way to the gallows. He said, "John P., do not cry. Today I will pay for what I have done, but thank God, I am about to receive the gift that comes from what God has done." Then he gave me his Bible. That was it. I lost it; I wept. I cried like a baby as I watched my friend—dead man walking.

—JOHN P.

CHAPTER TWELVE

INTENTIONAL YOU: CHANGING HOW YOU DO YOU IN RELATIONSHIPS

We are always in relationship with someone. Relationship is natural to us—we make it happen wherever we come into contact with others. The quotes above took place during my years of ministry in the maximum security block in H. M. Prison, Nassau, Bahamas. I was the counselor. Charlie D., John P., and I had forged a friendship around discussing scripture and other books. The relationship changed the three of us. That is the reward of building an intentional relationship—it changes who we are and how we behave.

BEHAVIOR #8: CHANGE

R10: POPULATE YOUR LIFE WITH INTENTIONAL BEHAVIORS.

How has relationship changed you? Is there a relationship that is changing you now? How?

The Greek philosopher Heraclitus wrote, "You cannot step twice into the same river." In several ways, that is also true of relationships. Relationships are always in motion. That is due to the fact that the people in them are always changing and growing. Tom changed. The years my team and I spent with Tom's team saw wholesale change in them and their employees.

We changed also—our approach to helping troubled teams since then has been to focus upon helping to heal relationships. Organizations are the sum total of multiple relationships; their outcomes result from how well people are changing and growing together in those relationships. In this chapter, the focus is upon facilitating and observing change and growth in your relationships.

So how *intentional* are you in your relationships?

An easy way to assess how intentional you are being in your relationship is to measure where you stand using the eight ongoing behaviors of an intentional relationship.

1. ARE YOU UPLIFTING? DO YOU MOTIVATE AND ENLIVEN THE OTHER PERSON?

Strongly Disagree	Disagree	Undecided	Agree	Strongly Agree
1	2	3	4	5

2. ARE YOU UNDERSTANDING? DO YOU CELEBRATE THE OTHER PERSON'S PERSONALITY?

Strongly Disagree	Disagree	Undecided	Agree	Strongly Agree
1	2	3	4	5

3. ARE YOU TALKING? DO YOU MAKE CONVERSATION WORTHWHILE?

Strongly Disagree	Disagree	Undecided	Agree	Strongly Agree
1	2	3	4	5

4. ARE YOU STUDYING? DO YOU EVALUATE HOW YOU RESPOND TO THE OTHER PERSON?

Strongly Disagree	Disagree	Undecided	Agree	Strongly Agree
1	2	3	4	5

5. ARE YOU SHARING? DO YOU CREATE AN OPINION-SAFE ENVIRONMENT?

Strongly Disagree	Disagree	Undecided	Agree	Strongly Agree
1	2	3	4	5

6. ARE YOU INFLUENCING? DO YOU INITIATE GROWTH-EVENTS TO HELP THE OTHER PERSON GROW?

Strongly Disagree	Disagree	Undecided	Agree	Strongly Agree
1	2	3	4	5

7. ARE YOU SERVING? DO YOU ACTIVATE THE GOOD IN THE OTHER PERSON BY DOING GOOD FOR THEM?

Strongly Disagree	Disagree	Undecided	Agree	Strongly Agree
1	2	3	4	5

8. ARE YOU CHANGING? DO YOU MONITOR YOUR BEHAVIOR TO ENSURE THAT YOU BUILD INTENTIONAL RELATIONSHIPS?

Strongly Disagree	Disagree	Undecided	Agree	Strongly Agree
1	2	3	4	5

How did you do? Did you score more toward Strongly Agree than toward Strongly Disagree? Whatever the total score is today, that is your starting point. It is what you should measure against in the next ninety days. Three months is enough time, if you are serious about building healthy relationships, for you to implement new intentional relationship behaviors at work and at home.

So what have we learned? We've already established that relationships are really like reflecting glass or a full-length mirror. One piece of glass, like a rearview mirror, for example, may be used to look at what we left behind. For some of us, there are broken people in our history, injured by us. For others, there are forsaken people, overlooked by us. Still others in that rearview mirror are healthy individuals, standing tall and proud because of our influence in their lives.

Relationships are like another piece of glass—a hand mirror. As we look at ourselves, we see the scars past relationships have left upon us. They taught us things. Maybe they taught us to be wary of people. Maybe they taught us to keep a safe distance from people. They taught us to shield ourselves. Or maybe in the mirror we see a happy face. One filled with the wonder of healthy relationships. Your smiling face reflects the support and focused attention you receive from your relationships. Or maybe in the mirror you see rippling muscles, borne out of the daily exercise you get from working hard on your relationships. You see the strong physique of putting yourself through the repetitions of lifting up your friends, family members, managers, and others. You see a healthy you.

Relationships are also like a magnifying glass. As you look through this glass at your relationships, you can see all the flaws. You see the disappointments the other person has caused you. You see the times when they did not remember the good things you did for them. You see the ways they may have betrayed you. You see their lack of interest or lack of engagement in the relationship. Before you choose to end such a relationship based upon what you see in the magnifying glass, do yourself a favor: please, turn the magnifying glass on your part in the relationship and look closely. Chances are, if you are honest, you see some of the same things from you toward them.

This brings me to the last of the promises I told you this book would teach you how to do: *to know when to terminate an unwanted or unhealthy relationship.* This is not a marriage counseling or career advice book. I do not presume to advise you to leave your spouse or your job. Those are very critical and personal decisions. So please use the following information *only* if you have made sincere and numerous attempts to reconcile with your spouse, friend, coworker, or supervisor.

If, however, you have decided to end your relationship, you must be resolute that none of the eight behaviors apply: The relationship is not *uplifting*; there is no desire to *understand* one another; *conversation* is destructive and hostile; *shared interaction* is at best as strangers and at worst as enemies; any *opinion* expressed fuels an argument; *influence* is null and void; you *bring out* the worst in each other; and neither of you are willing to *change.* This, then, is a relationship that has died, and all that is left is to enunciate the ways it fails to meet the standard of each and every one of the eight behaviors of an intentional relationship.

Finally, whatever piece of glass you need right now, take it in your hand, look into it, and know this: you are made to be in relationships. Relationships come with being human; they help us to be fully human. They exist to help you become everything that you are meant to be—but you must be intentional in your relationships to reap the greatest singular benefit they offer. That is the fully refined best *you.*

REFERENCE MATERIALS

EIGHT BEHAVIORS AND RIOS

BEHAVIOR #1: UPLIFT

BEHAVIOR #2: UNDERSTAND

BEHAVIOR #3: TALK

BEHAVIOR #4: STUDY

BEHAVIOR #5: SHARE

BEHAVIOR #6: INFLUENCE

BEHAVIOR #7: SERVE

BEHAVIOR #8: CHANGE

1. Evaluate the quality of the relationship by how you react to RIOs.

2. Renovate old thinking, about them and you.

3. Precipitate behavior change by what you say.

4. Educate yourself about the person's strengths and personality.

5. Create an opinion-safe relationship.

6. Instigate growth events.

7. Initiate selflessness by doing good.

8. Populate your life with intentional behaviors.

YOUR BEHAVIOR/INTENTION INVENTORY

1. What relationship is foremost in your mind right now? Why?

2. What was your intention when you started your relationship with _____?

3. How does your behavior today align with your original intention for your relationship?

4. What behavior do you want to be known for in your relationship?

5. What behavior do you need to change in order to enhance your relationship? Why?

INFLUENCE INVENTORY QUESTIONS

1. In the present situation, what value do I bring?

2. If I choose to withhold my influence in the present

instance, is any injury done to me, to others, or to the organization?

3. In the present instance, are others counting on me to influence their decision?

4. Is this a situation where others ask me to take charge?

5. When I have exerted my influence, in this type of instance, have I gotten my best results?

6. Are there instances or activities where I would gladly exert influence more often?

7. In my relationship(s) within the last six months, have I helped someone discover new opportunities for growth or increased success?

8. At work, is there a relationship where I have been reluctant or absentminded in my use of influence?

9. If I were given only one opportunity to influence, who would I influence to do what? Why?

PERSONAL INVENTORY

1. ARE YOU UPLIFTING? DO YOU MOTIVATE AND ENLIVEN THE OTHER PERSON?				
Strongly Disagree	Disagree	Undecided	Agree	Strongly Agree
1	2	3	4	5

2. ARE YOU UNDERSTANDING? DO YOU CELEBRATE THE OTHER PERSON'S PERSONALITY?

Strongly Disagree	Disagree	Undecided	Agree	Strongly Agree
1	2	3	4	5

3. ARE YOU TALKING? DO YOU MAKE CONVERSATION WORTHWHILE?

Strongly Disagree	Disagree	Undecided	Agree	Strongly Agree
1	2	3	4	5

4. ARE YOU STUDYING? DO YOU EVALUATE HOW YOU RESPOND TO THE OTHER PERSON?

Strongly Disagree	Disagree	Undecided	Agree	Strongly Agree
1	2	3	4	5

5. ARE YOU SHARING? DO YOU CREATE AN OPINION-SAFE ENVIRONMENT?

Strongly Disagree	Disagree	Undecided	Agree	Strongly Agree
1	2	3	4	5

6. ARE YOU INFLUENCING? DO YOU INITIATE GROWTH-EVENTS TO HELP THE OTHER PERSON GROW?

Strongly Disagree	Disagree	Undecided	Agree	Strongly Agree
1	2	3	4	5

7. ARE YOU SERVING? DO YOU ACTIVATE THE GOOD IN THE OTHER PERSON BY DOING GOOD FOR THEM?

Strongly Disagree	Disagree	Undecided	Agree	Strongly Agree
1	2	3	4	5

8. ARE YOU CHANGING? DO YOU MONITOR YOUR BEHAVIOR TO ENSURE THAT YOU BUILD INTENTIONAL RELATIONSHIPS?

Strongly Disagree	Disagree	Undecided	Agree	Strongly Agree
1	2	3	4	5

ENDNOTES

1. Bock, Laszlo. *Work Rules!: Insights from Inside Google That Will Transform How You Live and Lead*. New York: Twelve, 2015.

2. Seashore, Charles N., Mary Nash Shawver, Greg Thompson, and Marty Mattare. "Doing Good by Knowing Who You Are: The Instrumental Self As an Agent of Change." *OD Practitioner* 36, no. 3 (2004): 57. http://webmedia.unmc.edu/Community/CityMatch/EMCH/041907/ODP-Seashore%20et%20al.pdf.

3. Tripp, Paul. *What Did You Expect? Redeeming the Realities of Marriage*. Wheaton, IL: Crossway, 2010.

4. "intentionality." OxfordDictionaries.com, 2016. http://www.oxforddictionaries.com/us/definition/american_english/intentionality.

5. "intentional." Merriam-Webster.com, 2016. http://www.merriam-webster.com/dictionary/intentionality.

6. Bonsaksen, Tore, Knut Vøllestad, and Renee R. Taylor. "The Intentional Relationship Model." Scribd.com, May 2015. http://www.scribd.com/doc/272892428/The-Intentional-Relationship-Model#scribd.

7. Robinson, Lawrence, Joanna Saisan, Melinda Smith, and Jeanne Segal. "Bond with Baby: When and How it Happens." WebMD, April 20, 2015. http://www.webmd.com/parenting/baby/forming-a-bond-with-your-baby-why-it-isnt-always-immediate.

8. Steinfeld, Mary Beth. "Bonding Is Essential for Normal Infant Development." University of California Davis Medical Center. Accessed January 26, 2016. http://www.ucdmc.ucdavis.edu/medicalcenter/healthtips/20100114_infant-bonding.html.

9. Ertmer, Peggy A., and Krista D. Simons. "Scaffolding Teachers' Efforts to Implement Problem-Based Learning." Purdue University. Accessed January 26, 2016. http://www.edci.purdue.edu/ertmer/docs/Ertmer-LC05.pdf.

10. Ricucci, Gary and Betsy. *Love That Lasts: When Marriage Meets Grace*. Wheaton, IL: Crossway, 2006.

11. Chapman, Alan. "Personality Theories, Types, and Tests: Personality Types, Behavioural Styles Theories, Personality and Testing Systems—for Self-Awareness, Self-Development, Motivation, Management, and Recruitment." Businessballs.com, 2005. http://www.businessballs.com/personalitystylesmodels.htm#carl%20jung%27s%20personalit%20y%20types.

12. Beck, Randall, and Jim Harter. "Why Great Managers are So Rare." *Gallup Business Journal*, March 25, 2014. www.gallup.com/businessjournal/167975/why-great-managers-rare.aspx.

13. Tucker, Ken. *Intentional Conversations: How to Rethink Everyday Conversation and Transform Your Career*. Sanger, CA: Familius, 2015. Pg. 19.

14. Ibid., 23.

15. Clifton, Donald O., and Paula Nelson. *Soar with Your Strengths: A Simple Yet Revolutionary Philosophy of Business and Management*. New York: Dell Publishing, 1992. Pg. 121.

16. Covey, Stephen R. *The 7 Habits of Highly Effective People: Powerful Lessons in Personal Change*. New York, NY: Free Press, 2004. Pg. 255.

17. Martens, Judith. "Covey #5—Seek first to understand, then to be understood." Behavior-Change.net, July 16, 2013. http://www.behavior-change.net/covey-5-seek-first-to-understand-then-to-be-understood/.

18. "Item 7: My Opinions Seem to Count." *Gallup Business Journal*, May 3, 1999. http://www.gallup.com/businessjournal/502/item-opinions-seem-count.aspx.

19. Thompson, Kevin A. "Opinions Rarely Matter." Kevinathompson.com, April 3, 2014. www.kevinathompson.com/opinions/.

20. Ibid.

21. "Recognizing Good Performance, Characteristics of Good Recognition, Coaching: An Approach to Solving Performance Problems and Giving Constructive Feedback." Enrollment Services Training, Staff Development and the Work-Study Office, Boston University.

22. Patterson, Kerry, Joseph Grenny, David Maxfield, Ron McMillan, and Al Switzler. *Influencer: The Power to Change Anything.* New York, NY: McGraw-Hill Book Company, 2008. Pg. 4.

23. Ibid., 7.

24. Fairless, Benjamin. "Serving Others." Foundation for Economic Education. National Conference of Christians and Jews at Los Angeles, April 26, 1956. www.fee.org/freeman/serving-others/.

25. McLeod, Saul. "Maslow's Hierarchy of Needs." SimplyPsychology.org, 2014. http://www.simplypsychology.org/maslow.html.

26. Luke 6:38, New Living Translation of the Bible.

ABOUT THE AUTHOR

As a thought leader, **KEN TUCKER** brings many years of being a highly sought-after speaker and principle consultant, formerly with The Gallup Organization, then as strategic consultant and CEO of Ken Tucker and Associates, LLC, and now as a senior partner at TAG Consulting. He is the author of *Intentional Conversations* (Familius, 2015), coauthor of *Animals, Inc: A Business Parable for the 21st Century* (Warner Books, February 2004) author of *Are You Fascinated? The Four People You Need to Succeed* (Dailey Swann Publishing, August 2009), and coauthor with Kevin Ford of *The Leadership Triangle*, and coauthor along with Todd Hahn and Shane Roberson of *Your Intentional Difference: One Word Changes Everything*. He is a regular contributor to management columns.

ABOUT FAMILIUS

Welcome to a place where parents are celebrated, not compared. Where heart is at the center of our families, and family at the center of our homes. Where boo-boos are still kissed, cake beaters are still licked, and mistakes are still okay. Welcome to a place where books—and family—are beautiful. Familius: a book publisher dedicated to helping families be happy.

VISIT OUR WEBSITE: WWW.FAMILIUS.COM

Our website is a different kind of place. Get inspired, read articles, discover books, watch videos, connect with our family experts, download books and apps and audiobooks, and along the way, discover how values and happy family life go together.

JOIN OUR FAMILY

There are lots of ways to connect with us! Subscribe to our newsletters at www.familius.com to receive uplifting daily inspiration, essays from our Pater Familius, a free ebook every month, and the first word on special discounts and Familius news.

BECOME AN EXPERT

Familius authors and other established writers interested in helping families be happy are invited to join our family and contribute online content. If you have something important to say on the family, join our expert community by applying at:

www.familius.com/apply-to-become-a-familius-expert

GET BULK DISCOUNTS

If you feel a few friends and family might benefit from what you've read, let us know and we'll be happy to provide you with quantity discounts. Simply email us at orders@familius.com.

Website: www.familius.com

Facebook: www.facebook.com/paterfamilius

Twitter: @familiustalk, @paterfamilius1

Pinterest: www.pinterest.com/familius

THE MOST IMPORTANT WORK
YOU EVER DO WILL BE WITHIN
THE WALLS OF YOUR OWN HOME.

CPSIA information can be obtained
at www.ICGtesting.com
Printed in the USA
FSOW01n1517210416
19530FS